# PREHISTORIC ROCK ART

## OF COUNTY DURHAM, SWALEDALE AND WENSLEYDALE

STAN BECKENSALL AND TIM LAURIE

COUNTY DURHAM BOOKS, 1998

County Durham Books are
Durham County Council's
Arts, Libraries and Museums Department



First published 1998
ISBN 1-897585-45-4

# Foreword

**BY RICHARD BRADLEY, PROFESSOR OF ARCHAEOLOGY, UNIVERSITY OF READING.**

Not so long ago I had the good fortune to be given leave from my university so that I could study the prehistoric rock carvings of Britain and Ireland. I had seen some of these sites before, but the splendid examples on the moorland around Barnard Castle were quite new to me. I was lucky to be guided round these sites by the authors of this book. The two days that I was there were among the most enjoyable that I have spent in the field. The rock carvings were at once impressive and enigmatic, and the landscape in which they are set full of interest. Not only did they contain many monuments of the same age as the rock carvings; they were among the few areas of Britain to preserve other evidence of how the people who had made those images used to live.

This book brings back memories of visiting these remarkable places. It evokes the peculiar character of the sites and the surrounding country in an extraordinarily vivid way, and it helps to place the rock art itself in a wider context. There is plenty here to set the imagination free. The authors have recorded a little known aspect of our past and made it available for us to enjoy. I hope that you, the reader, find the experience of seeing the carved rocks as exciting as I did myself. The prehistoric past may seem remote from our daily lives, but the traces it left behind are for everyone to share. In every sense this book leads the way.

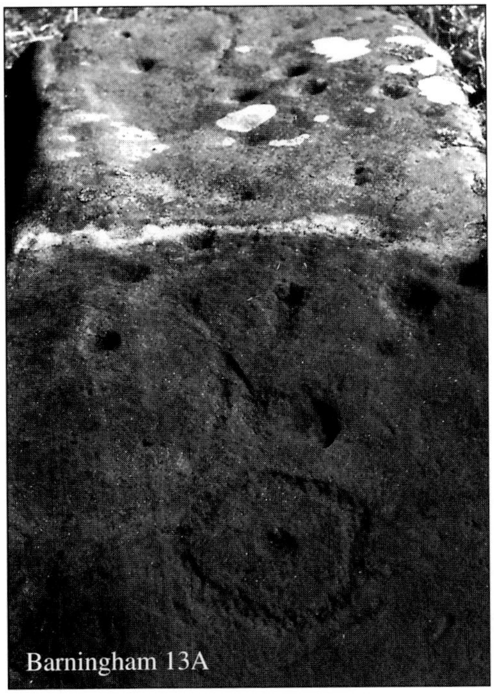

Barningham 13A

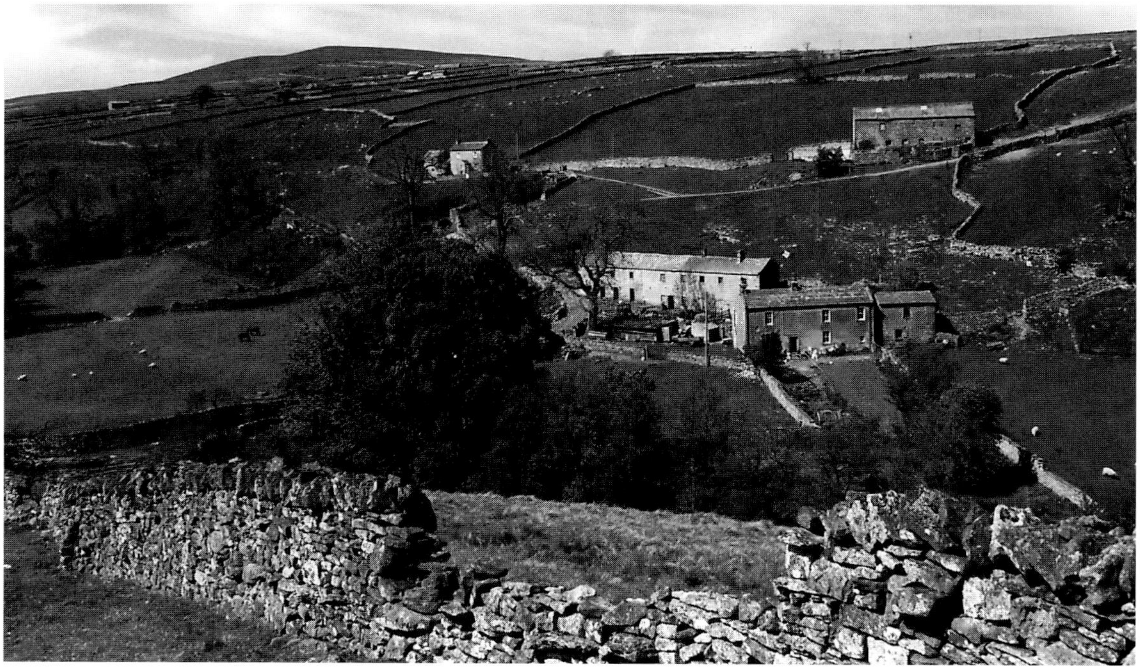

ROCK ART COUNTRY: Holgate Moor rises above Helwith Farm, on the horizon.
Bottom: The broad floor of the Marske Beck.

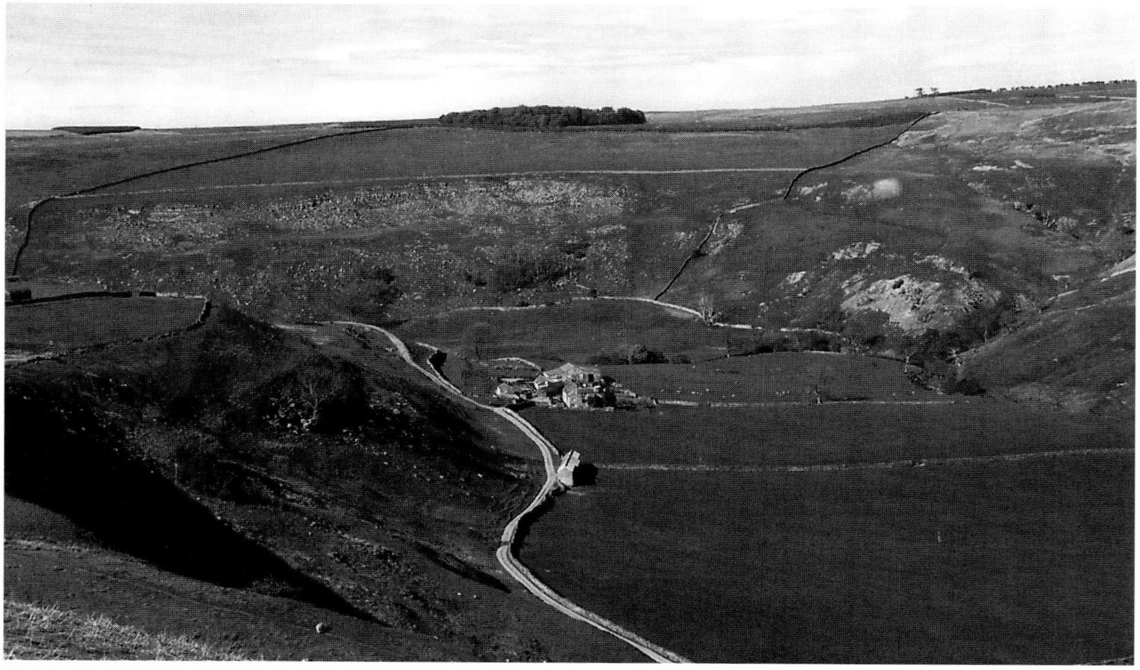

# Contents

# Access to Rock Art Sites

Readers should be aware that many of the rock art sites described in this book are on private property and there is no permitted public access. Where possible, access arrangements are referred to in the text. Anyone planning to visit any of the sites described in this book is urged to check carefully rights of way by consulting up-to-date Ordnance Survey maps or by contacting the County Council Rights of Way Officer. Many rock art sites are found in upland areas which are also grouse moors. Especial consideration and care should be given to visiting these areas during the nesting season from late March to May and during the shooting season in the months following August the twelfth.

Those requiring more information on rock art sites are encouraged to contact the relevant County or National Park Archaeology Officer who will both be pleased to assist you and learn of any new discoveries of rock art.

It is hoped that this book will lead more people to visit the museums where rock art is displayed locally. Both the Bowes Museum at Barnard Castle and the Old Fulling Mill Museum of Archaeology in Durham City have notable examples on display.

County Archaeology Officer
Arts, Libraries and Museums Department
County Hall
Durham
DH1 5TY

County Archaeologist
Heritage Unit
Environmental Services
County Hall
North Yorkshire
DL7 8AH

Archaeology Officer
Yorkshire Dales National Park
Yorebridge House
Bainbridge
Leyburn
North Yorkshire
DL8 3BP

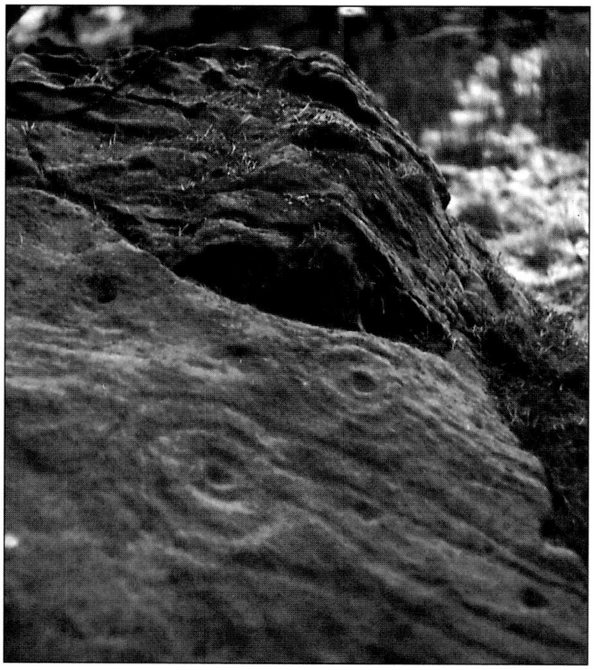

Gayles Moor

# Introduction

Most of the rock art in this book has been recognised during the last 30 years, although it may have been seen, but unrecorded before. We use the term 'art', as others do now, because its presence enhances the landscape. It is in the 'cup and ring' tradition, and unlike mobile artefacts such as tools and pottery, it is more or less permanent and fixed in the landscape setting. It is a visible and tangible link in time and place between us and our aboriginal ancestors.

When we set out to write this book we did not realise fully how many motifs there were; many have been recognised for the first time during this research. Look at any work on prehistoric rock art before this, and you will see that the area we cover was void of known rock carvings. New publications are beginning to redress the balance. As yet, however, there is no formal or popular account in this area, and we have to fill in that ourselves. It's not that no work has been done: it's more a question of bringing it all together and making it available.

The choice of prehistoric rock art as a major contribution by Durham County Council and the Northern Rock Building Society to Visual Arts Year, 1996, opened many eyes to the fascination of these ancient symbols among visitors to the exhibition, and stimulated the modern artists who were commissioned to present their response to 5,000 year old art. A day's conference at Durham, arranged to present the findings of specialists on northern rock motifs within its international context, was very well attended, and brought together Professor Bob Layton and Professor Richard Bradley, Stan Beckensall and Paul Frodsham as speakers.

We have a problem, though, in presenting our work to you, because the subject attracts at different levels both specialists and those with a general interest in the landscape. We have to write accurately and in sufficient detail to interest other specialists, and at the same time share the delight of this subject with a less specialised, but equally demanding readership. We also have an essential obligation to put rock art into a background of general prehistory so that it takes its rightful place not as a fringe activity, but as a vital component in people's development. We may not succeed in satisfying everyone! One of our best assets is that rock art is visual, and we have devoted half the book to drawings and photographs. At least there is something for everyone there, although illustrations cannot convey the sense of time and place.

We also have an obligation to those who own the land, who use it, and who make their living from it, to help preserve their rights, so we ask our readers not only to observe the 'Country Code', but to ask permission if you wish to visit those sites not on public rights of way.

The book has been written in our own time, as a hobby, and at our own expense. Tim Laurie has been living and working in the area for many years, and has made many of the site discoveries. He has been concerned with the initial recognition, survey and recording of archaeological sites of all periods in the landscape of Teesdale, Wensleydale and Swaledale. Stan Beckensall has now finished the very lengthy task of recording accurately every panel of known rock art from the Scottish border to Wensleydale, which has been published in 6 books and many articles. It has been an ideal partnership, each learning from the other so that more people can build upon this work. A wealth of data is now available, but the question of understanding and interpreting, and indeed further discoveries, will continue for years to come. Even then many questions may remain unanswered regarding these motifs.The study of rock art has at last been established as a serious academic discipline. Recording methods have been developed and applied thoroughly, and the increased interest shown by many archaeologists, both amateur and professional, together with the public, is continuing to help in the discovery of more sites. The raised public and professional awareness, we hope, will encourage official bodies paid by us through our taxes to work out effective ways of preserving and caring for these important cultural and landmark features. From our work we hope you, the reader, can see the remarkable sites that exist in the field. We would hope you join with us and judge that they are worth preserving.

Addleborough Cairn

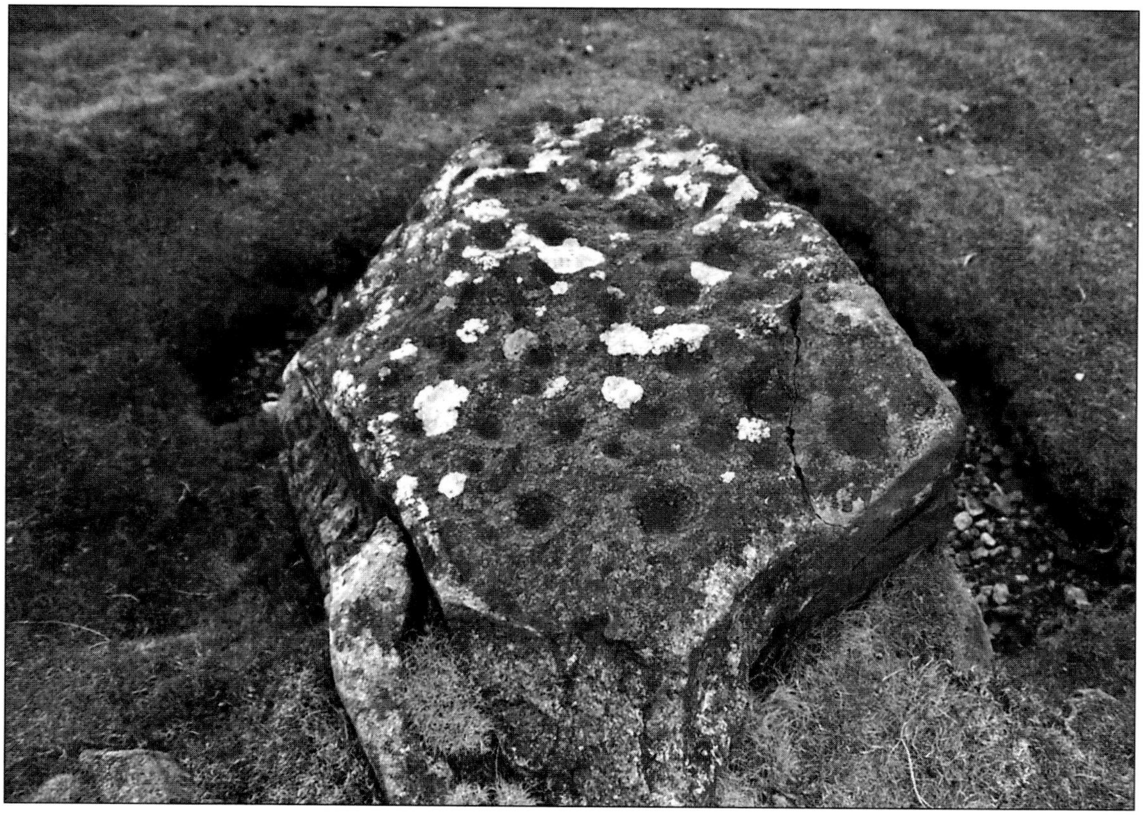

MAIN ROCK ART SITES FROM EGGLESTON TO JUNIPER GILL.
This sketch map shows the access roads to the sites, high ground and rivers. Villages and small towns are initialled. Solid squares show the areas of rock art. At Winston, a removed portable is indicated by a hollow triangle, and solid triangles at Ravensworth and Silver Hill (east Gayles) indicate portables.

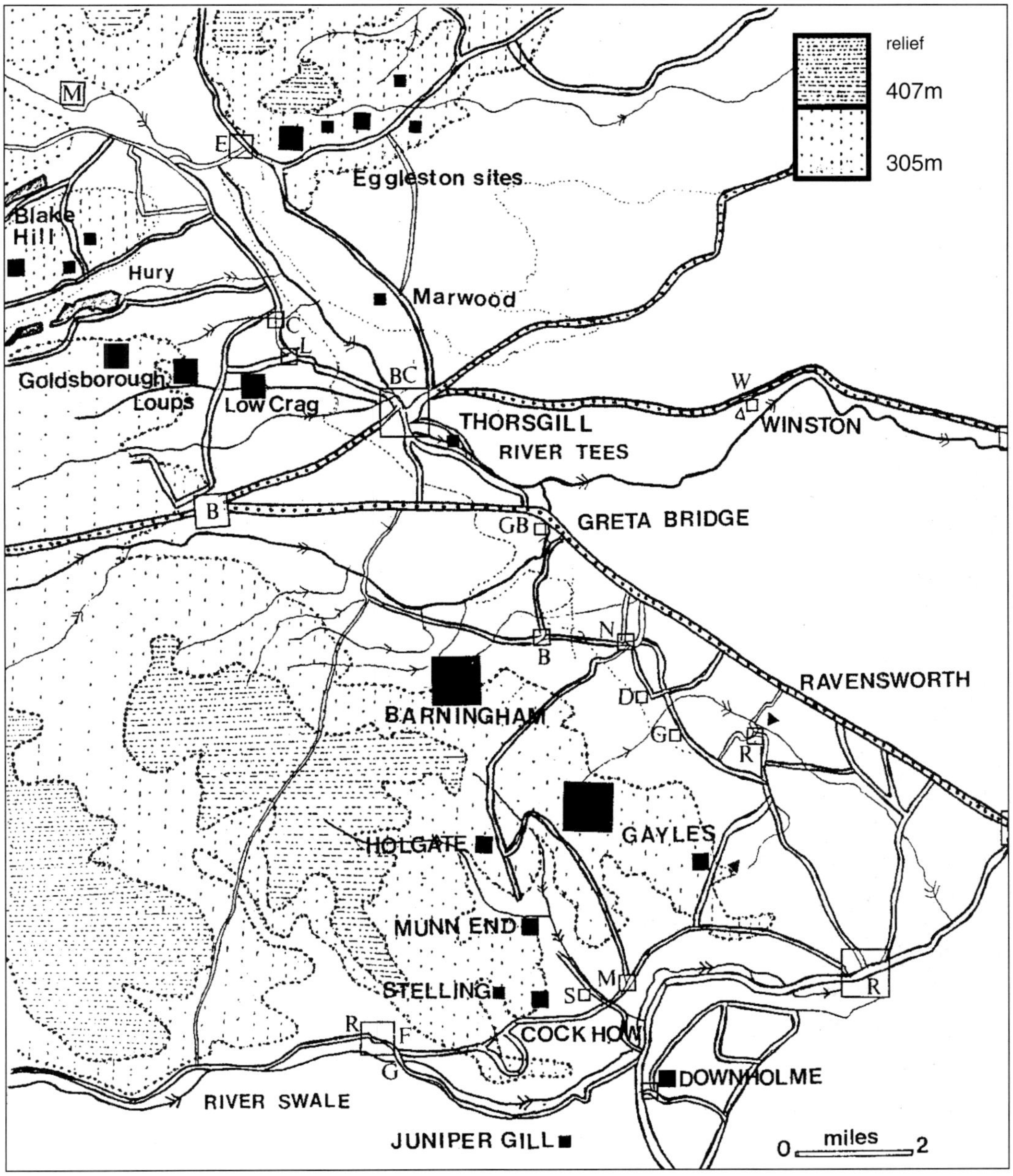

# 1. The Archaeological Background

Before we can understand the position of rock art in the landscape, we have to see it not as isolated or impulsive graffiti, but as part of a wider picture of landscape use in prehistoric and later times. We look at all the places where people have left traces of their activities, whether it be of people roaming the landscape in search of food, of herdsmen, settlers on arable land, of people burying their dead or building henges, stone circles or other ritual monuments. We discover that surviving prehistoric landscapes can be extensive, including field systems, settlements (farmsteads, village-like groups of houses, paddocks and tracks), and ritual or burial complexes. The earliest evidence for human activity from our area is that of Middle Stone Age (or Mesolithic) cultures, hunters and gatherers who used arrows tipped with minute stone points called microliths, made of flint and chert, and they were active across and within the areas where rock markings have been found . They were living their nomadic lives until about 5,300 years ago, and beyond. There is a hint of the presence of late glacial hunters on gravel terraces near the Tees and in Wensleydale before these Mesolithic people.

This kind of life was gradually replaced or supplemented by pastoralists, who relied more on herding animals. Rock markings are found in areas where both the hunters and pastoralists operated. The motifs were made on rocks on high ground overlooking the river plains or on bluffs and glacial terraces close to the rivers. The markings are not found at intermediate heights at any distance from the rivers. Before the markings were made, the regions had already been used by people who had a long tradition of surviving in a wilderness which can be assumed to have been rich in food such as game animals that provided skins, fur and meat, many game birds, and fish, especially migratory salmon.

It may be assumed that the markings were made in a pristine wilderness as yet altered little by human activity. The evidence for hunter groups is very scant, and limited to small scatters of flint and chert tools, for these are all that survive below acid peat and in the gravel soils of ploughed river terraces. These traces have been found in only four locations in Wensleydale, two of which could have been visited by the same group of hunters. In Swaledale and Teesdale there is more evidence, but the sites are limited in distribution and the tools show that the sites were probably visited for only one or two nights and re-visited only occasionally over long periods of time.

This sporadic and limited visiting of a site can be explained, for following the final retreat of the ice sheets there is a 4,000 year period during which there was a rapid extension of woodlands dominated by birch, pine and hazel. The landscape from coast to hilltops became almost completely covered in forest. All the evidence suggests that the main year-round settlements during this time were on the coast or close to it. Britain became an island only 8,000 years ago when the North Sea finally removed the land bridge that connected us with Europe. Before this, the Pennines were a range of hills on the edge of a vast north European Plain and shallow sea. Hunter gatherer groups here may have shared culture and technology with groups in north Germany and southern Scandinavia.

This very brief outline simply introduces the idea that people existed in the area long before the markings were made. Later we shall look at the difficult question of when rock art was made and the strong link of that rock art with much later cultures. Firstly let us turn our attention to where within our study area rock art is found.

There is only one site in the whole of Wensleydale, a cup-marked round barrow on the top of Addlebrough. There are none in Upper Swaledale, west of Reeth or in Arkengarthdale. In Teesdale, no markings exist on suitable rock surfaces which abound across the whole of Scargill Moor, and only one small boulder has come from Stainmore. No sites have been found so far in Upper Teesdale, west of Eggleston, in spite of comprehensive 'field walking'. None has been found anywhere above 500m.OD. In the lowland zone, nothing exists at any distance from the river.

In Teesdale most marked rocks occur in open clusters or groups of individual sites above 250m OD on the highest slopes that form the southern edge of the Tees valley, now unenclosed heather grouse moor or rough pasture. The main groups, from east to west, are followed in detail in this book, and consist of: High Hag, Feldom and Gayles Moor, Barningham Moor, Cotherstone Moor, and above Deepdale. A group has recently been found east of Eggleston, with others also above 300m OD at Bracken Heads, Blake Hill and Marwood. A few isolated marked rocks have been found on river terraces or bluffs immediately overlooking the Tees and Greta, at Gainford, Egglestone Abbey and Greta Bridge. Their importance will be emphasised later.

In Swaledale the markings are confined to rough pasture and heather moor just below or above 300mOD, in the vicinity of Marske Beck, a principal north bank tributary of the Swale. These sites occur in small groups at Cock How, Munn End, and Skelton Moor, and on the SW. slopes of Holgate How. An isolated cup and ring marked rock is at Lower Stelling close to Dales Beck. Finally, there are three small rocks with cups and grooves on Downholme Moor near Thorn Hill, south of the Swale, and above Juniper Gill on Ellerton Moor is a cupped standing stone that marks a pass or saddle between Swaledale and lower Wensleydale.

This disjointed and patchy distribution pattern provides a concrete link between the developing and increasingly successful farming communities of the late Neolithic (New Stone Age), Bronze Age and Iron Age, who were our settled ancestors, and the aboriginal hunters of the very distant past. A close correlation can be observed in the location of areas preferred for Middle Stone Age hunting sites and the areas with rock markings. Swaledale and Wensleydale appear to have been rarely visited, let alone permanently occupied until the pastoralists arrived and constructed the first monumental earthworks: henges, round barrows and cursus monuments in the Vale of Mowbray (at West Tanfield, Boroughbridge and Catterick), and in the Vale of Eden (with some well known sites such as Long Meg and the Mayburgh henge, the former having some very impressive markings).

The presence of rock art in Teesdale and on the Tees-Swale watershed may be accounted for by the fact that this area is close to the natural routes on the Teesdale southern slopes which would be followed by a traveller on foot moving between these great Neolithic monument complexes. The markings are on the margin of land available to transhumant pastoralists whose main settlements were probably on the Tees, Swale, Ure lowlands within the vale of Mowbray. However, no rock markings have been found in the vale of Eden except on Neolithic monuments. An interesting pattern in Cumbria as a whole is that almost all rock art is associated with monuments.

As readers will observe and as has been previously noted, the majority of rock art sites are to be found in upland areas. Questions may be asked of why the sites are concentrated in such situations. Aside from the intentions and ritual needs of the people who created the monuments and which are

A wide range of Flints from sites in Teesdale and Wensleydale

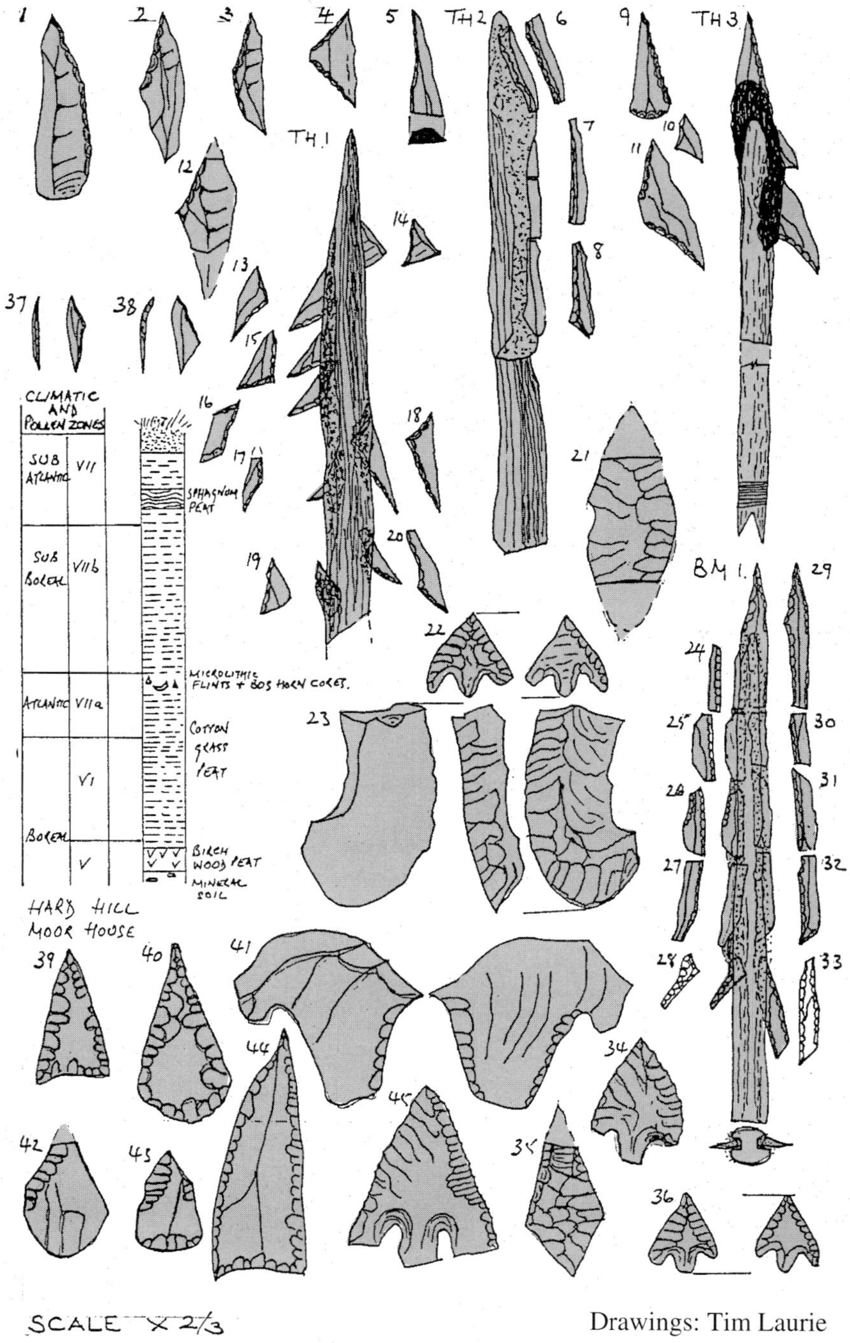


Drawings: Tim Laurie

discussed elsewhere, there are a number of more practical factors are at work here. Firstly, such areas have an abundance of suitable rock for marking, both as free-standing boulders and earthfast bed rock. Secondly, because of the altitude and remoteness of these areas, they have suffered less disturbance from farming and building over the last three millennia than many low land areas. The presence of individual rocks at low elevation at Egglestone Abbey, Gainford and Greta Bridge, and the large number of motifs from other lowland settings such as Witton Gilbert, show that at one time rock art may have had a much wider distribution. It is, however, likely that the upland areas always had a preponderance of such sites, and it is here that study is perhaps best directed where motifs still exist in some numbers, in-situ and in association with other field monuments such as burial cairns and stone circles.

ARTEFACTS:

No archaeological sites exist in isolation and the totality of evidence from a landscape is immensely important. The preceding page of drawings illustrates the range of stone implements found within two miles of rock art sites. Although not all contemporary with the rock art, these may give an idea of the tools available to the peoples culturally associated with the development and use of rock art.

They are listed as follows:

A. Mesolithic and Neolithic flints from Teesdale (Nos. 1-38) and Wensleydale (Nos. 39-45)

B. Nos 1-23 Towler Hill
Nos. 24-36 Barningham Moor
Nos. 37-8 Hard Hill, Moor House National Nature Reserve.

C. Peat column diagram, after Johnson and Dunham, 1963.
Nos.39-41 Semerwater
Nos. 42-45 Thornton Rust Moor

D. Reconstructions:
Spear and knife (TH1 and TH3), after Desmond Clark, 1959, but with microliths from Towler Hill.

E. Loshult-type arrow with microliths from Towler Hill (TH3)
Bone point with microlithic flint inserts from Barningham Moor, after Juras Barta, 1985 (BM1).

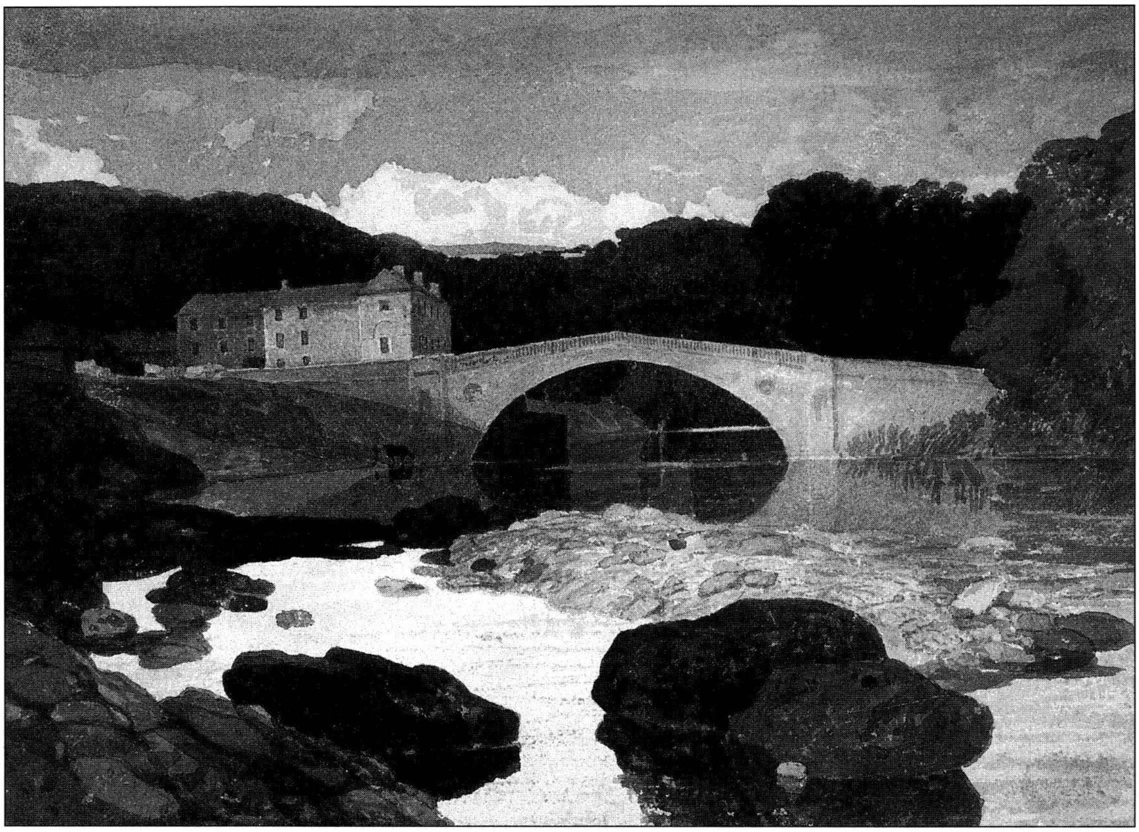

Greta Bridge
John Sell Cotman
© British Museum

# 2. Views of a Landscape

Through the search for rock art, we can see the landscape through different eyes. Until now we have been concentrating on its significance in the past, trying to people the past, trying to understand how the land was used and settled in prehistoric times. The landscape can also be looked at as a thing of beauty, and our knowledge of how and why it has been changed may add to that enjoyment.

To appreciate the view of another person from a different time from our own, we can look at the landscape of the Tees and Greta through the eyes of a painter. John Sell Cotman was inspired by his visit to J.B.S. Morritt's great house, Rokeby, in July and August 1805 to paint views of the area including a watercolour of Greta Bridge. We see a single arch stone bridge over the Greta, painted at river level some 200m. below the bridge and just above where the east abutment of the modern concrete bridge of the A66 by-pass now stands. This modern road was partially constructed on the old Roman street running east-west across the Stainmore Pass. The beautiful cambered and rutted surface of the Roman road was revealed during excavation prior to the building of the new road.

Within the painting we see, in the near view, Greta Bridge and the courtyard coaching inn, cattle drinking, and the river through the wide-span arch emerging from the wooded ravine of Brignal Banks. There is a faint distant horizon above the trees formed by the southern edge of Teesdale-Barningham High Moor, the How Tallon Ridge. With the eye of faith we might even discern the prehistoric barrow itself as a faint rise or dimple. Cotman repainted this view after a visit to Paris and was influenced by fashionable neo-classical romantic landscapes, and his second version, at present on view in the Morritt Arms at Greta Bridge, shows a distant snow-covered Alpine mountain!

Many years were to elapse before How Tallon was excavated, with the results reported elsewhere in this book. In 1897 the Reverend Reginald Alfred Gatty was sitting on the mound eating his lunch during a day's shooting, and recognised his picnic site as a burial structure. Together with his host Sir Frederick Milbank, he called for spades and picks, and the next two days were spent digging. Burials, pottery and flints emerged and were taken away. Marked rocks were left on site unnoticed and were later to be built into a stone wall across the mound, where they were recorded for this book.

This mound overlooks an area where rock art is present on numerous surfaces, but there is another link with Greta Bridge. There was a Roman fort there which may have been called Maglona, still visible behind the Morritt Arms. It was in the Roman period that a decorated prehistoric slab was found, re-used as the cover of a Roman grave at the roadside some 500m. east of Greta Bridge. This slab is now at the Bowes Museum, and recorded elsewhere in this book.

In a way then, the Cotman painting brings together place and the people who have used it and savoured it over time. It is a metaphor, and the relationship between different land forms continues with different uses: from the nomadic hunters and pastoralists of the high moorlands to the inhabitants of the well-drained, sheltered fertile lands on the gravel terraces now occupied by the great houses at Rokeby, Mortham and Wycliffe, and once by the Roman fort at Greta Bridge. Modern and Roman roads follow the valley, and prehistoric trackways and paths over

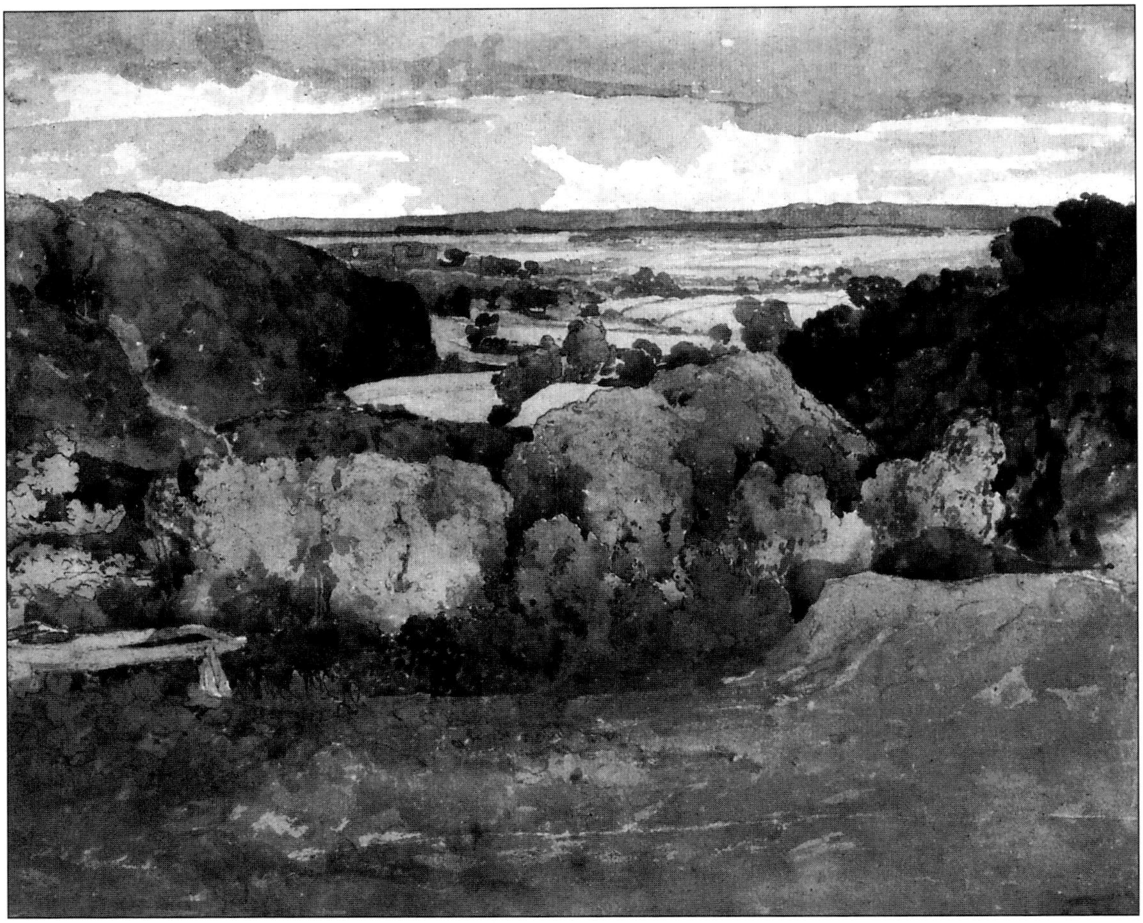

Barnard Castle from Towler Hill
John Sell Cotman
© Leeds City Art Galleries

the Moor survive as the Badger Way.

Cotman's painting of Barnard Castle from Towler Hill in 1805 provides a second stimulus for reflection. The view is to the distance across the Tees lowlands and to the south east of Barnard Castle, with a dark horizon formed by the low hills of the Tees-Swale uplands. In the foreground is a prominent bend and low fall of the Tees where the river has cut through hard sandstone cliffs and has been diverted by this obstacle to form a series of "ampitheatre" terraces after the final retreat of ice 15,000 years ago. It is an accurate watercolour of a scene largely unchanged today.

The gravel terraces through which the Tees runs hold the evidence of early prehistoric settlement spanning thousands of years, revealed in flint and chert scatters where the plough has removed all other traces of earlier settlement. At Cotman's view point of Towler Hill are the fire-cracked cobbles from cooking hearths or pits. The rock art sites look down upon such lowland settlements, but very occasional slabs decorated with cup and ring marks have been found in these low areas, such as at Egglestone Abbey, Gainford and Greta Bridge. The lands favoured for permanent settlement were not the areas where rock art is found in any quantity. So the landscape that we see today in the most fertile areas was cleared thousands of years ago of its forests, land was ploughed and farms established, and the pattern since has been the continuous use of the same land, destruction and rebuilding going on constantly. But the high moorlands, never suitable for arable, and today used only for marginal land and shooting, retain surface evidence of their prehistoric use.

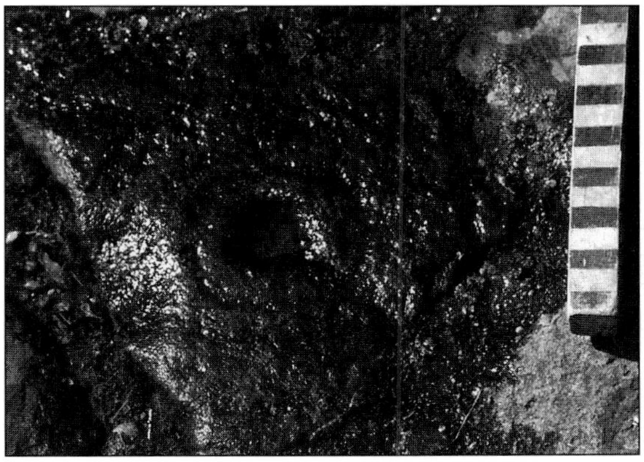

Ravensworth

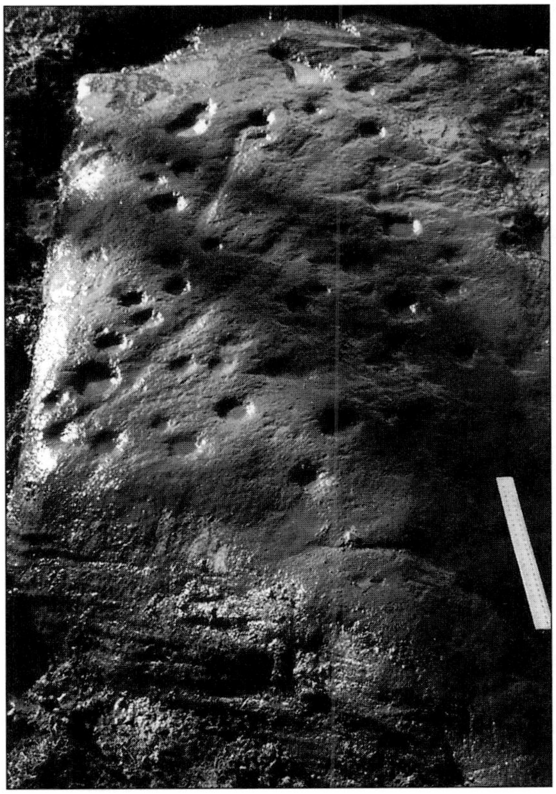

Low Crag, Deepdale 1

# 3. Symbols on Stone

## Living off the land

We live in a world in which so many of the resources of the planet have been exploited that we find it difficult to go back mentally to a time when people's needs were, in comparison, simple. The amount of accumulated rubbish thrown out each week contrasts with the sparse fragments of what Prehistoric people left behind, such as pottery, tools, the things lost, or the objects deliberately buried with their dead or left as some sort of votive offering. Although the underlying rocks of the landscape remain untouched, apart from quarrying, the soils and vegetation have changed considerably since people began to roam the landscape in search of food and shelter. Today we are very aware of the results of pollution and of over-exploitation of the world's resources. Never before has this happened on such a large scale.

Yet people have always used what is around them in order to live. For thousands of years this meant gathering plants in the wild, whatever was edible, and eating whatever flesh became available. Some particularly useful plants might be encouraged to grow, and agriculture would slowly develop, with a chance discovery pushing the process on. The more food there was, the more people could live and multiply, and the more people interfered with the vegetation and animals, the more changes would take place in the appearance of the land.

## Back in time

About 5,000 years ago, the time that we are concerned about in this book, people had already cleared areas for the growth of crops, herded some animals, and hunted others. The success of their growing crops depended on the fertility and depth of the soil, the climate at the time, the height above sea level, and their experience in coping with these factors and using the land to its best advantage. People who were farmers, hunters and herdsmen were fully aware of how they depended on the land, and they observed the movement of sun, moon and stars and the cycles of procreation and birth in the animals and crops that kept them alive with a sharpness that we may have lost. We think of them being "close to nature".

We can only imagine how different life was for them, and look for things that we might still have in common. Our material lives could not be more different, yet we imagine that they experienced joy, frustration, a deep sense of loss when someone they cared for died, love, hate, pain and relief. We also know that they spent a disproportionate amount of time building what might be called by a materialist "useless" buildings, structures that had no practical value in producing food or other wealth. We see ditched enclosures, and standing stones, long and round cairns, all expressing a need to be in touch with ancestors, or with each other in a re-affirmation of their tribal identity, and of the need to have a special place to which they could turn. We have a "cool web of language" that we hope will keep away some of the awful (and aweful) thoughts that beset us. Some reach out for horoscopes today, swing needles on cotton above pregnant women to predict the sex of the child, have faith in the national lottery despite the astronomical odds, welcome a black cat or avoid walking under a ladder. Our superstitions and our inadequacies take many forms. Some things do not change!

If we can imagine then, people living five thousand or so years ago, moving across the landscape of lightly forested uplands overlooking the richer, more fertile but densely-forested river valleys, knowing from signs and shared memory the best places to fish, to hunt, farm and gather, we may also see them not as vague Mesolithic or Neolithic people but as individuals who depended on each other. Among these people some were brighter or stronger than others, some had greater insight into other's psychology...you will have your own thoughts about this, but we can agree that not everyone would have been the same.

When something unusual happens to us we mark the event, not only in our memories, but often physically. A war produces a mass of memorials, and their symbols are recognisable and widely understood: a cross, a soldier leaning on his rifle, for example. Although the Christian tradition of this country has declined, the church building still attracts gatherings to mark the 'Rites of Passage': baptisms, weddings and funerals, and in crises people may return to some half-forgotten sanctuary. Within that building, depending on our religion, we may expect to find at least one cross, and its symbolism does not need to be explained to us. All religions have their symbols, instantly recognised. At a more worldly level, we are surrounded by logos. The National Parks have their curlew, the National Trust its acorns. There are so many symbols that we just accept them. Some of them are useful because they simplify an operation for us; following pictures can be easier than following words. Others hide a wealth of meaning that can be of great importance, like the cross, that most potent of all symbols in Christian churches.

When we try to tell people about the most important things that happen to us -about pain, about love, about yearning for something lost or missing, -we find it almost impossible to express this simply. Prehistoric people chose to express their observations about life and their view of the world by symbols marked on rock surfaces. They have left us no evidence of their language or writing and only through trying to "read" their paintings and other forms of art can we have any idea of what was going on in their minds. This may however present a great heap of problems! A painting of a hunted animal, with its grace, power and speed may tell us about what was around at that time, but it can also tell us that the painter admired these qualities in the natural world, and even that he would have liked to have such attributes himself. Some paintings are 'naturalistic' but in others there are symbols that can't easily be explained. Why is it that young children early in their development draw people with extended arms and legs? Why do they go through the same stage of selecting some attributes of human beings and rejecting others? We can go into our friends' houses where such art is displayed on the kitchen wall and remember that we have seen it many times before. Their art has selected the most important things that they see around them.

The best works of art are not those that merely reproduce a kind of photograph of what is seen. We have different ways of seeing a place or a person. The phrases "Beauty is in the eye of the beholder"; "I can't see what he/she sees in him/her" are familiar to all of us. We all look at life with different eyes, based upon our experience and the refinement that we develop. The child who sees a petrol stain on a wet road as a melted rainbow may perceive life at that moment quite differently from an anti-car campaigner. If we can see a part of life through the eyes of children, by being prepared to listen and to look, we may be in a position to understand that primitive art is well capable of selecting what is most important in life, and expressing it.

## The World Picture

Rock art world-wide takes many different forms, but we know that over 70% was produced by hunters and gatherers. Over 150 major rock art sites have been identified, representing over 40,000 years of history, and a large part of these are in desert and semi-desert, isolated today. We can see lively hunters pursuing game, dressed in ritual head-dresses and other 'symbolic' clothes, procreation and fertility well-represented, weapons flying through the air, horses, chariots and ploughs, bees buzzing around a honey gatherer, primitive boats... the time span is great and its distribution so widespread that this art includes all forms of human activity.

When we get to Durham and the Dales, how can we see this art form against such a world picture? One really striking fact stands out: we have no human figures, no animals, no implements: only abstract motifs. Even then, in the rest of Britain, the odd hand or foot print add up to very little. Axes and daggers on Stonehenge or at Kilmartin are unique. Another striking observation is that the symbols used in our area are the same as those used all over Britain. No matter what differences there are on panels of rock art, the people were using the same basic symbolic language. Some were more articulate than others, if you like, and perhaps the more sophisticated among the motif-makers attract us more than those who decided on a simpler form of expression that carried a different kind of message. There are some forms that are rare and lie outside normal 'cup and ring mark' art, principally spirals of different kinds, and there are none of these in our area.

## Discovery and a search for meaning

'Cups and rings' have been known for nearly 200 years in Britain. In neighbouring Northumberland a historian called Tate recorded in the second half of the Nineteenth Century:

" Mr. J.C. Langlands discovered some worn and defaced figures incised on a rude sandstone block, near to the great camp on Old Bewick Hill in north Northumberland. Though strange and old-world looking, these figures then presented an isolated fact, and he hesitated to connect them with past ages, for they might have been the recent work of an ingenious shepherd, while resting on the hill; but on finding, some years afterwards, another incised stone of a similar character on the same hill, he then formed the opinion, that these sculptures were very ancient. To him belongs the honour of the first discovery of these archaic sculptures."

A Durham connection is then made in the form of that famous antiquarian and canon of Durham Cathedral, the Rev. William Greenwell, who in 1852 read a paper at the Archaeological Institute of Newcastle on the subject. Unfortunately the paper was lost and never published. In 1867 Sir James Simpson of Edinburgh published the Scottish sites. Since then, interest in the subject has simmered gently, with few professional archaeologists venturing into the unknown, but now the subject has been brought to the boil. The main areas have now been published in some form or other. In the rest of the world, the interest in the subject and the resources allocated to it are making up for neglect, and seeking to stop the disappearance of what is now recognised as an essential and unique part of our heritage. It gives an insight not only into how people used their environment to make a living, but how some places took on a special importance in a religious/spiritual way. As Mr. R.J. Lampert says of the Australian Aboriginals:

"While the extent of a territory was known, boundaries were less important than sacred sites, usually natural features in a landscape where spirit ancestors had performed creative or other heroic deeds, the re-enactment of which ritual, by succeeding generations, maintained the relationship between people and land and ensured the replenishment of natural resources."

Let us put that another way and apply it to our own area. People need to define which areas they think belong to them so that they don't conflict with each other. For that reason territory is

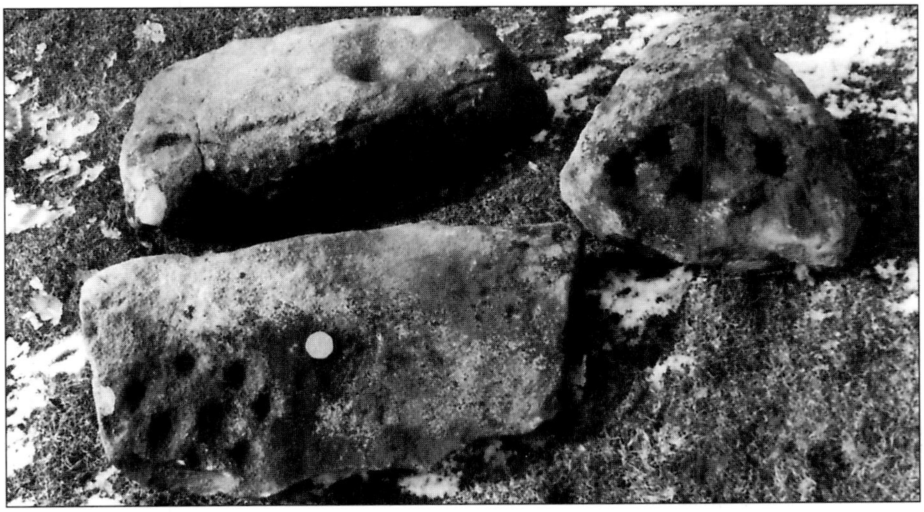

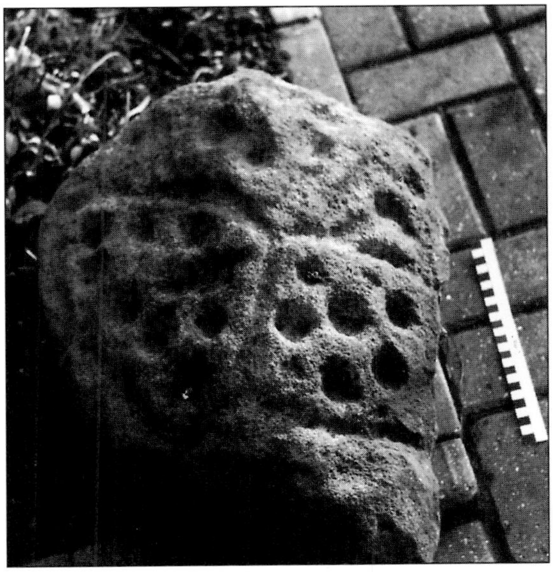

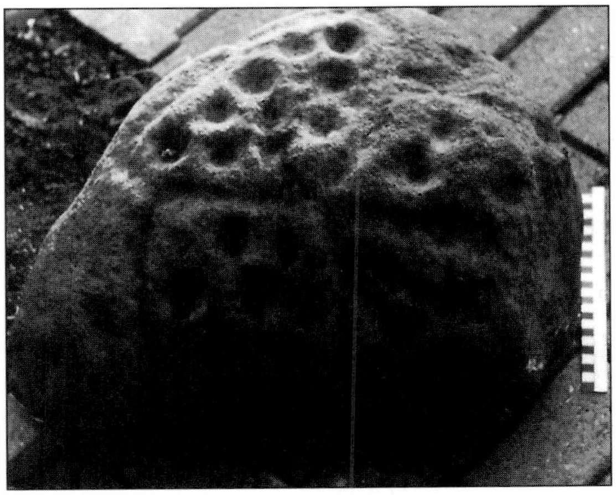

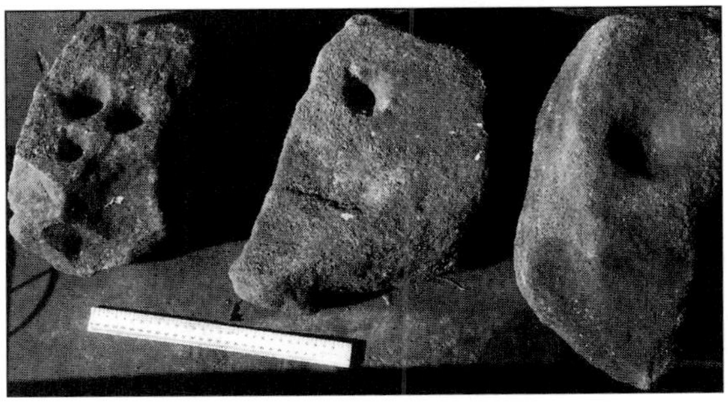

"PORTABLE" STONES:
top right. How Tallon
above and mid right: two views of Witton Hall Farm stone.
Bottom : Low Crag

marked out because each group needs so much in order to live. That becomes especially important when population increases. Such boundaries were not confined to farmed land; there were hunting areas too. One can imagine the people on Gayles Moor and Barningham looking out across their territory, knowing its limits, but at the same time remembering someone for a feat of strength, a particularly fine and dangerous or successful hunt, or the death of one of the tribe. These sites were marked and reminded people of their ancestors, but they also reminded people that they couldn't take the land for granted. Catastrophes could happen, when the weather turned nasty, when animals didn't breed well, when disease struck. People knew that there were forces outside themselves which controlled or affected their destiny, forces that had to be respected, propitiated with gifts and bribes perhaps. Rituals might have developed to ensure that the right things were done at the right time. There were circles of soil, and ditches, wooden posts, stones, burial cairns of different kinds where not only the ancestors resided but the 'gods' too. Just as some people today may hope that salvation will come from space, ready with superior intelligence to sort out the mess that we have made, so primitive people might look to a spirit world for guidance or help. All hope for 'divine' intervention. The spiritual world would have existed inside them, and it would have been possible to tap it if one only knew how to! Shamen would enter such a spirit world, and come back to offer guidance, through tokens that the spirits provided, to the tribe.

This is, of course, speculation. We don't really know whether Prehistoric people thought this way, but we have to use whatever analogies we can from the world that we know in order to begin to understand. We have a common humanity, but a very different background!

## Finding what we like

The trouble with symbols, when their origins and meanings are unclear, is that we tend to read into them whatever we like. One of the authors, in the early days of his search for meaning, had spent some time in Malta where the spirals on megalithic temples were strong growth images, and the temples contained some representations of a fat fertility goddess. Fertility is crucial to survival, so we would expect this to be stressed by people who live 'close to nature', and find its way into their symbols. There are lots of examples in world-wide primitive art. The concentric circles and their penetration by ducts might be seen as an expression of sexuality/fertility, but that does not mean that they were. Your first impressions have to be questioned: are you reading into ancient symbols something that is not there? Most people see a circle as 'eternity', with no beginning or end, but how do we know that people in the past saw it in that way? There have been over a hundred interpretations of these symbols teased out by Ronald Morris, including musical notation, sacred cowpats, family trees, star charts and maps, and this is a reminder that we should be looking for an explanation that can be supported. The trouble is that we don't know for sure how the symbols originated or what they meant. Perhaps the people who used them didn't know how they originated, but with the same symbols used in graves and in the landscape, the carvings surely were not random graffiti.

Although we can't give a definite explanation, this should not stop us from opening up our minds to possibilities, provided we don't say definitely that this is what they are or how they 'worked' in the landscape or on monuments. The act of walking the land to see already-discovered motifs, and the search for new discoveries is an exhilarating experience, for we can enjoy the whole landscape and its mystery. So if artists want to use these symbols in their own work or poets to write about them, why not? After all, art can only be experienced through individuals.

## What do you see?

Ronald Morris' "One hundred and four varieties" of explanations were included in his book, "The Prehistoric Rock Art of Galloway and the Isle of Man" in 1979. It was an informative and amusing excursion that resulted from his reading and from his many contacts with people as fascinated as he was by the origin and meaning of the symbols. As a solicitor, he weighed the evidence and awarded them marks out of 10 on their possible conviction.

He supported Professor Thom's arguments that some were placed on standing stones that had important astronomical alignments. He noted their use or re-use in burial mounds. One of his strongly-held beliefs was that their proximity to copper and gold ore had some significance, although this does not work in most parts of Britain. He was strongly convinced of their religious and magical significance, and not at all moved by theories that they denote breasts, the Mother Goddess, eyes, and phallic symbols, or that they are connected with fertility rites. He pointed out that there was no evidence to link them to sun worship, water divining, their use as mixing vessels, for casting bronze or colour, quantity measures, or the Freemason's earliest symbol, the All-Seeing Eye!

Copies of worm-casts, tree rings, and ripples made by stones thrown into water were given very low marks. Druids don't come into it because they didn't exist then, and the idea that blood was poured into the carvings isn't supported by any evidence. Their use as clocks was dismissed. Messages from outer space and early writing were rated zero. The authors are not convinced that many are based on megalithic inches. Other theories listed by Mr.Morris include bonfire ritual site markers, an aid to seed production, early pilgrimage marks, dye and transfer moulds, maps of the countryside, building plans, star maps, and a tattooist's shop window.

Although he dismissed suggestions that the carvings were placed where they are in course of some sort of search of food, and gave it 2/10, we now believe that there is a convincing case here, and that they could be boundary markers of sorts (1/10) and route markers. Could they be merely decoration? Doodles? Could they have been games? Do they represent parts of animals? Are they primitive lamp bases? Water images? Among the explanations that he dismissed completely were their use as secret treasure maps, plans for megalithic structures, for mazes, field ploughing plans, victor marks, early masons' marks, marks made by adders coiling up on the rocks, an early form of musical notation, a tuning device whereby wise men could alter the pitch of a rock's natural vibration by carving it, a locked-up force, worship of the sea goddess, markers for healing wells, children's art, or just natural marks. The rest of his researches brought in oath marks, knife-sharpening marks, early astronomers' night memoranda, and inclusive birth-growth-life and death symbol, healing magic, a mirror with its handle, and a womb symbol.

This is by no means the end of speculation. One article referred to the symbols as family trees, and such departures as rectangles were meant to represent bastards! It will go on, of course, and allow people their flights of fancy. But acceptance of any theory, including any put forward by the authors, would have to be supported by evidence.

A recent theory to account for the universal use of the symbols, irrespective of the time they were made, is that they are 'Entoptic' imagery. This means that all people have common images locked into the central nervous system, and that various stimuli can release the images. In primitive communities, such as the Bushmen of Africa , the shaman will go into trance and describe experiences in the spirit world by drawing spirals, concentric circles and wavy lines. Similar imagery is common among Australian aborigines. However this is only one of many unproven theories.

## Realising what we know

Despite all uncertainties, there are some things that we do know, such as the rough time span for their use, a knowledge of how the motifs were pecked onto the rocks, the precise places where they are found. We can record them accurately, and compare types of motifs not only in Britain but with the rest of the world. We also know that as well as those set on earthfast or outcrop rock in the landscape, there are others in a ritual context with monuments such as burials and standing stones, and that they can be transferred from one site to another.

## Preservation

Sadly, some recorded rock art has disappeared. The use of the land for farming or quarrying means that its surface is vulnerable. Cairns are destroyed, and their stones built into walls, rock is quarried for building and if there is no one aware that there are motifs on it, or no one cares, the motifs disappear. Natural agencies such as frost and rain erode the patterns. We tend to think that rock surfaces endure for ever, but all surfaces weather and motifs on exposed surfaces can weather away quickly after the removal of protective vegetation. Grass and sedge roots can penetrate the surface of open-grained sandstone. Weathering processes are complex, and rock art that has survived for over four thousand years may now be adversely affected by acid rain. So who is to look after it? Who decides whether a vulnerable surface should be removed from public view by covering it so that it doesn't erode any more? Is there a compromise to be made in which some sites are kept open as examples in the field? Should replicas be made, and the original site covered with artificial rock, and should replicas be displayed in special centres or museums? Britain is not alone in facing such problems, and in some hot countries where the art is painted on rock the situation is more critical. Little or no action has been taken to preserve and display rock art in Britain, and where it has, the provision of an iron fence around it to keep off sheep and cattle may prevent further damage, but destroys the atmosphere. What we hope that this book will do is to make more people aware of what we have, and hopefully we can work together to help solve the problem of conservation and display.

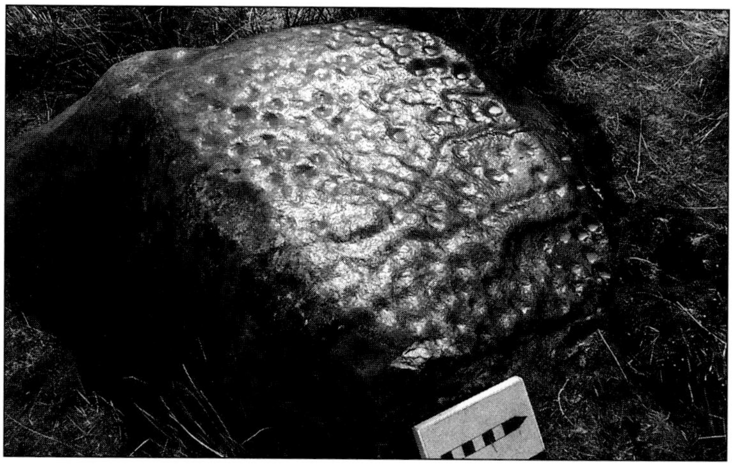

COCK HOW ROCK 3

# 4. Symbols and Motifs

The simplest symbol in rock art is called a "cup", a circular depression made in the rock with a pick. A "groove" is another symbol. When these symbols are combined, they are called "motifs". Thus a cup and ring together form one of the most common motifs.

Where the rocks have been freshly excavated, and from others, we know that the motifs were pecked into the rock surface with a hard stone tool that leaves each individual pick mark behind. Some may have been ground smooth afterwards, but as exposure to the elements can also produce this effect, we cannot be sure. If a mark is made on a rock with a knife-like cut, this is known as an incision, but this technique was not used in this region. The most likely way of pecking/picking a rock with control over the pointed tool would be by impacting the tool with a mallet. Something like a deer antler could also be used as a pick. Some tools had large, blunt points, and others had delicate nail-like points which could be used for marking out the design or to make particularly fine cups and grooves.

The shape of the rock, and any natural depressions already on it might suggest how to use the surface. Otherwise, the reasons for the choice of a particular rock are unknown to us. It may have been the only one uncovered at that time, or its place in the landscape may have had a special significance, such as the view from it or for an event that took place there.

It is usually impossible to say whether markings on a rock were made all at once, or over a period of time. Some designs appear unified, and others consist of random motifs.

There now follows an analysis of the way the symbols and motifs were arranged.

**CUPS**: Most cups are about 5cm in diameter, and only about 2cm deep, but some exceptions are so big that they become "basins". They may appear singly, grouped randomly, or arranged in patterns such as dominoes or circular clusters.

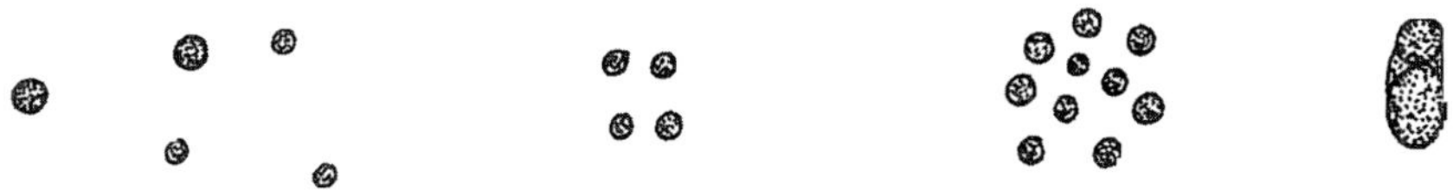

Two cups may be joined together to form an oval. Cups may be joined together by a straight or curved groove. Some grooves are made by joining cups together, either as lines running down a rock or as circles.

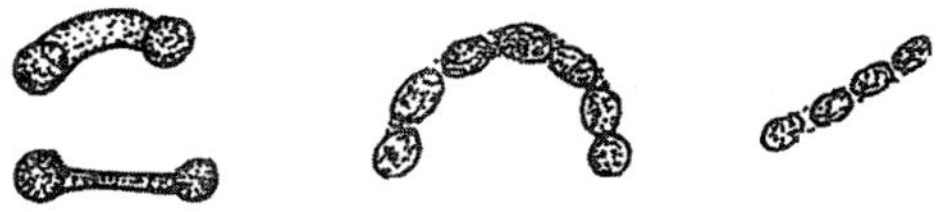

Frequently, cups are central to a design, notably at the centre of one or more concentric circles, usually with a straight groove leading out of the circles from the cup.

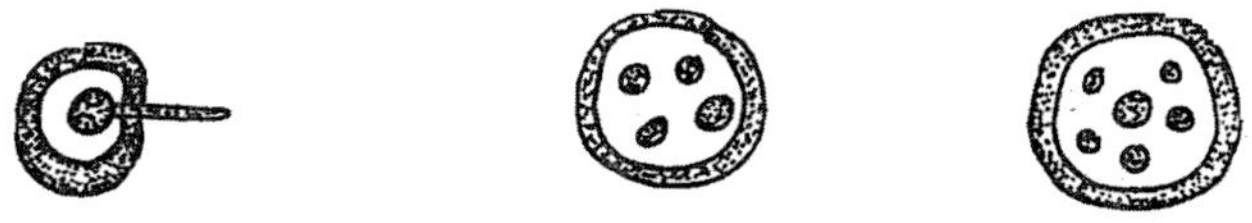

A number of cups may be enclosed by a groove, in one rare example as a rosette pattern, in which a cup is central in a circle of cups.

**GROOVES.**

A combination of cups and grooves is what produces the distinctive "cup and ring" marks, but there are examples of enclosures formed by grooves with no cups involved.

These are the common motifs:

cup with penannular

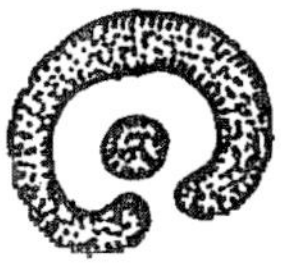

cup and ring

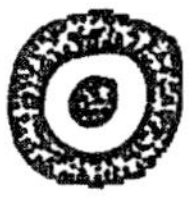

cup with multiple penannulars

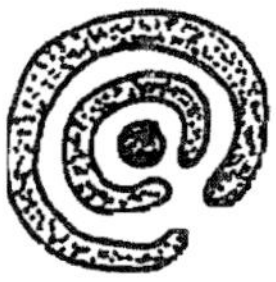

cup with multiple rings

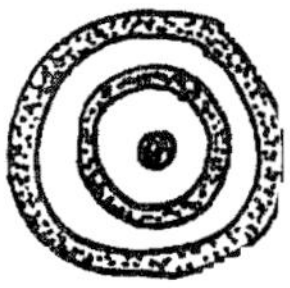

cup, groove and penannular

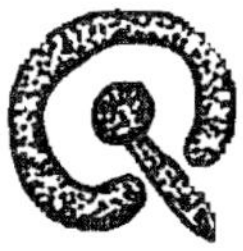

cup, groove and ring

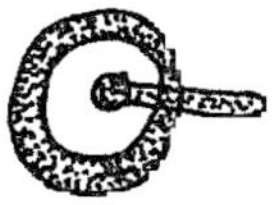

Rare motifs:

cups enclosed by a ring

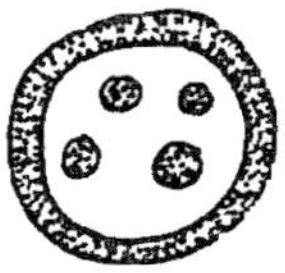

rosette enclosed by a ring

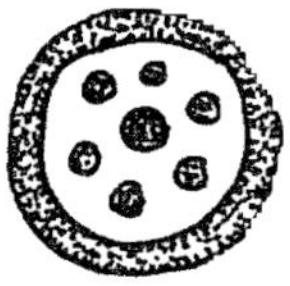

double groove enclosure

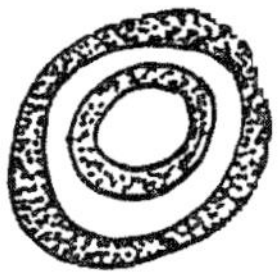

heart-shaped grooved enclosure

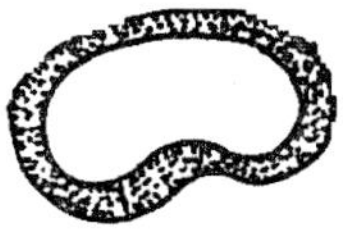

V-shaped enclosure

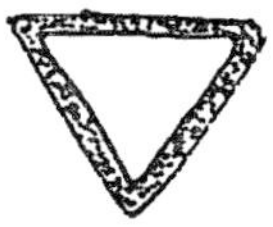

keyhole type

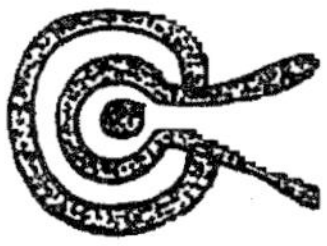

The simplest way of classifying the motifs and symbols in this region is:

1. Cups only
2. Cups and linear grooves
3. Circular and penannular grooves enclosing cups
4. Cups, linear grooves, circular grooves, penannular grooves

# 5. Recording Rock Art

There are many ways of recording rock art. In the past many beautiful and inspired drawings and lithographs were produced, which, although attractive artistically, were not always accurate depictions of what was actually on the rocks. Recording today makes use of a variety of techniques, amongst which photographic recording in ideal lighting conditions is essential. The second essential method is to produce an accurate scale drawing.

There are many areas of controversy, especially when any method is proposed that may damage a rock surface. This survey has made use of wax rubbing on thin newsprint on dry rock. Drawings are then made by placing a squared grid over the rubbing, and copying the details onto squared paper. The result is checked carefully with photographs and videos. The drawing has to show the relationships of motifs on the same rock, and the subtleties of how the cups and grooves were made. For example, linear and curved grooves may be pecked out with little variation in the width and depth of the groove, but many are made of touching cups, or by joining a string of cups together like beads on a string. In the latter case the drawing must show this process. Another example: when a cup lies at the centre of a group of concentric rings, and has a groove leading from it, it is important to show whether the radial groove precedes the addition of rings or whether it cuts through the rings after the rings have been made. The drawing must demonstrate the technique of the maker in as much detail as possible, and show unfinished and tentative efforts, and fainter, perhaps earlier use of the rock.

The recorder must take into account the same factors that influenced the choice of rock and the incorporation of surface features into the design. A rock is not a flat canvas, yet a drawing represents it as such. This is why it would be ideal to have a drawing always accompanied by a photograph. There are essential constraints in recording. The most important is that substances such as chalk should not be used to highlight the motifs, partly because a chemical reaction can damage a rock, and because we are forced to see what someone else thinks is on the rock. Although in arid lands the use of water to enhance a pattern on the rock is forbidden, this constraint can hardly apply to areas where the rocks are being rained on all the time. The most difficult problem is lichen and other growths, and whether their removal will do more damage to the rock than the organisms themselves. We advise that the rocks should not be touched at all. Most are scheduled Ancient Monuments and protected by law.

## Where Rock Art Occurs

There are five main types of rock in this region where rock art occurs;

1. On earthfast slabs: these have been moved from local or distant outcrop by ice-plucking action.
2. On earthfast boulders: these are glacial erratics, and are often rounded and scratched.
3. On outcrop rock
4. On portables: these rocks have been moved from their source by people who have incorporated them into structures, such as a burial cairn. Portables may, of course, be removed from the structure where they were originally deposited
5. On a standing stone.

All motifs in this area are on fell sandstone of

Carboniferous age. Lake District volcanic erratics and erratics of Shap granite occur in considerable numbers in Teesdale, but no motifs have yet been found on them.

## Details of the Technique of Recording

The two rocks drawn here are on Gayles Moor, and as they are both important and accessible, they are described here in detail as an example of recording.

**Rock D 9.**
What the drawing does not show, but the photograph does, is that the rock is a gently-rounded earthfast sandstone slab.
At the centre, where a number of grooves join, the strike of the rock radiates outwards. Some of the very fine natural cracks have been utilised as grooves, some well-defined, others faint.
A decision was made that the circular groove (RHS) surrounding a rosette of cups (the central cup with a groove running out of an already established line from the centre) should be linked to the rest of the motifs on the rock by two main grooves, one from the centre of the rock, and the other leading towards another dominant motif: an ellipse containing 4 cups. The drawing shows how the main groove that links them together forms a distinct panel that includes cups and a faint cup and ring. There is a deep cup inside this panel round which the main groove curves.
What the drawing does not show is that the type of pecking that produced the linking groove and the rosette and ellipse was probably made by the same tool.
The fluidity of grooves, which vary in depth and width, ending in, or starting from some cups, also exclude other cups, which remain isolated, some strong and others faint.
On a near vertical part of the boulder (LHS), a little space has been filled with a huddle of cups and single rings, not all deeply executed, where they seem to jostle for position.

**Rock D 4**
This is an earthfast slab, with its marked surface near vertical as it juts out of the ground, part still buried.
The surface must have been originally uneven, and may have determined the pattern of the motifs.
The drawing shows how the grooves run down the slope of the rock (top to bottom), linking many cups, and there are also some grooves coming in obliquely. It also shows that the cups vary in size and shape. Some are ovals. Some have incomplete rings around them.
On the RHS is a good example of central cup, penannular, and a groove leading into a larger cup, then on to the end of the rock. Around this integrated figure are unconnected cups.
What is obvious from the drawing is that cups predominate: they are deep, assertive, and linked by thin linear grooves.
The drawing's faint dotted lines indicate incomplete, tentative grooves, perhaps a rough-out. Perhaps there was already so much packed onto this rock that they called it a day!
The dotted line at the base indicates ground level, and there may be more under that.

Although to modern eyes one rock has a more sophisticated design, both exhibit an interesting use of material available, with slope, strike, and surface irregularity playing their part. Both confirm that the tools used to produce the designs were blunt stone chisels, for the individual pick markings are clearly visible. As this was the standard tool throughout Britain used to produce motifs, I have used a stippled filling in the grooves to re-create that idea, but only in a 'decorative' way.

The drawings speak for themselves.

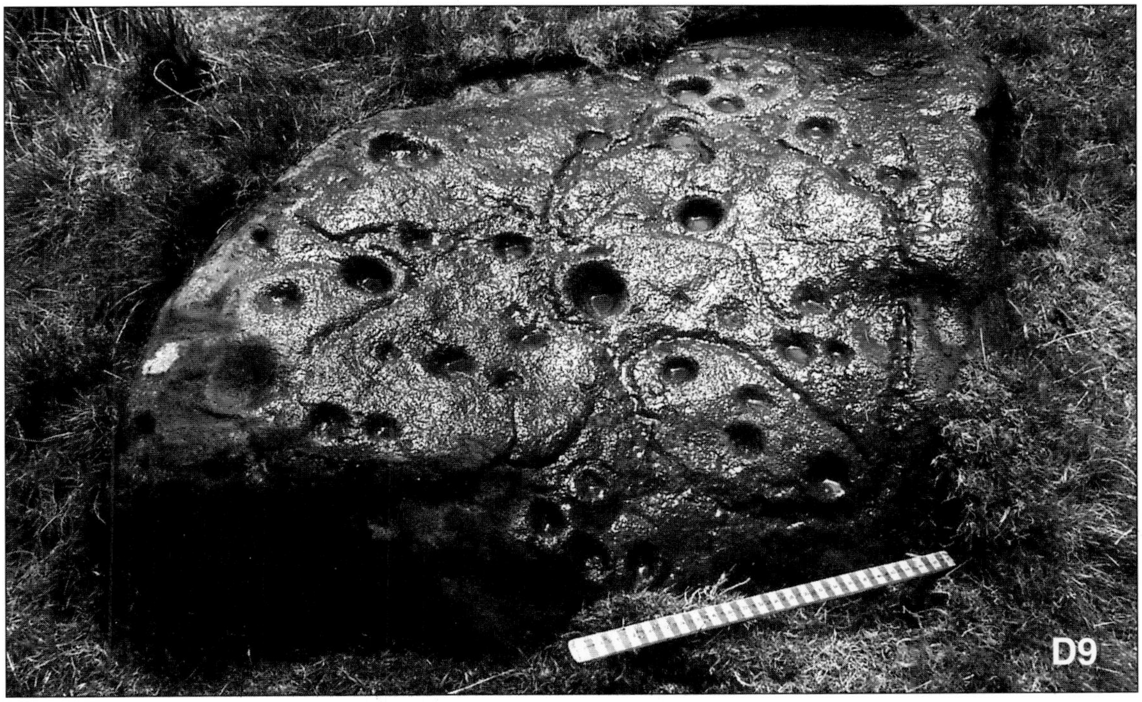


THE PHOTOGRAPHIC RECORD
Two earthfast rocks on Gayles Moor, with a centimetre scale. Compare these pictures with the drawings.

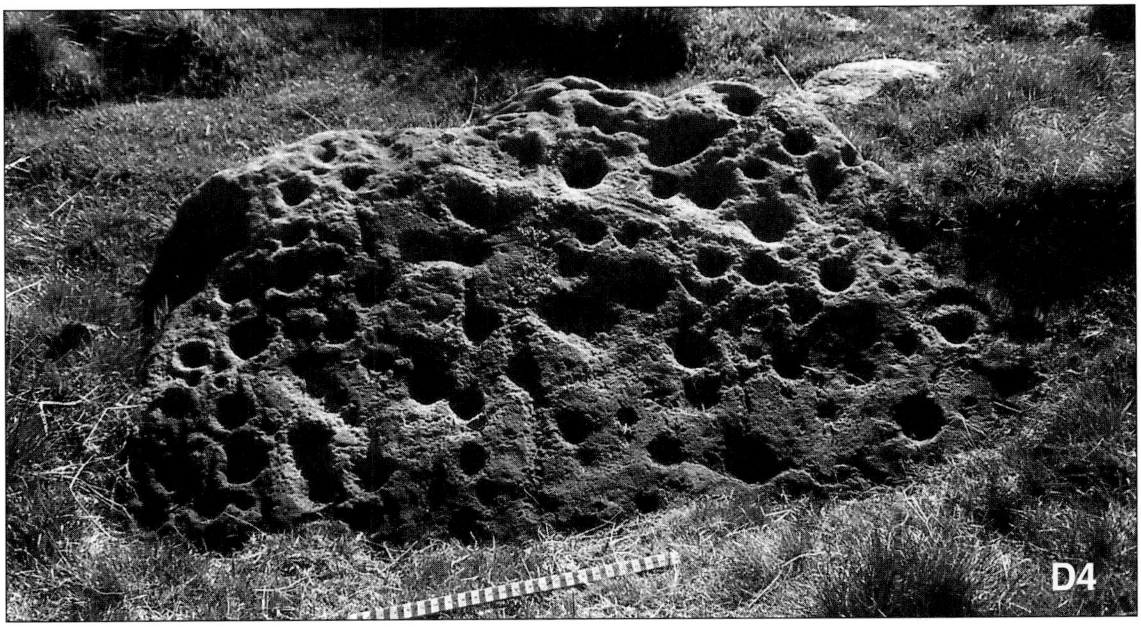

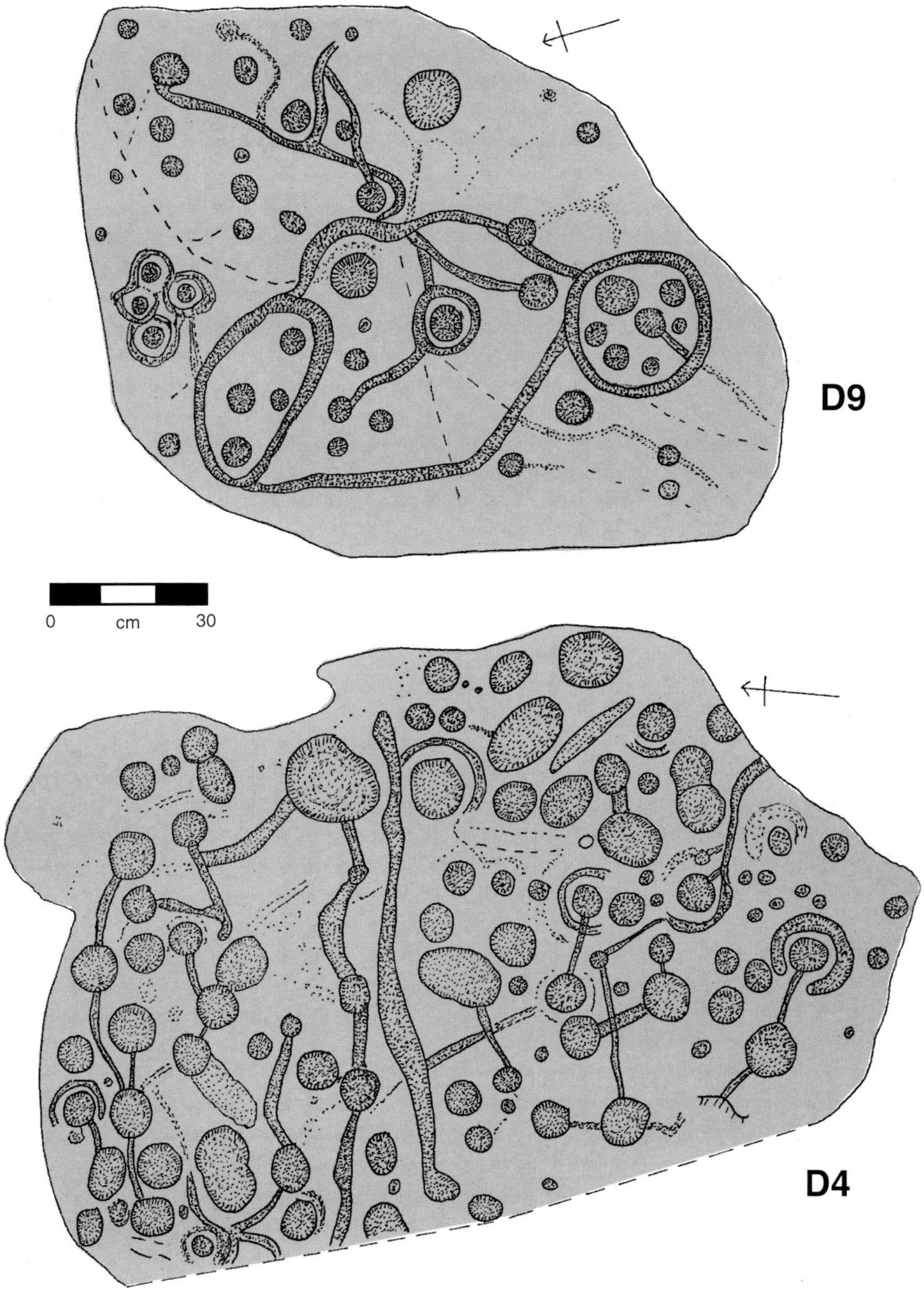


Gayles Moor D9 and D4

Fulforth Farm

Cist cover

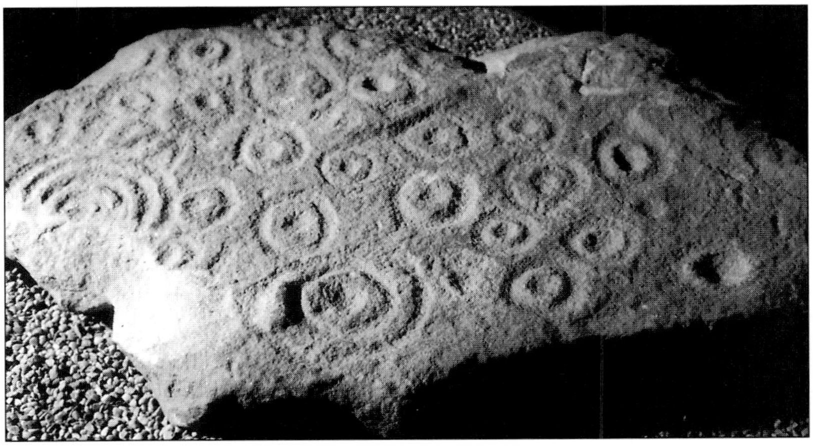

Marked flat stone in the Cist pit

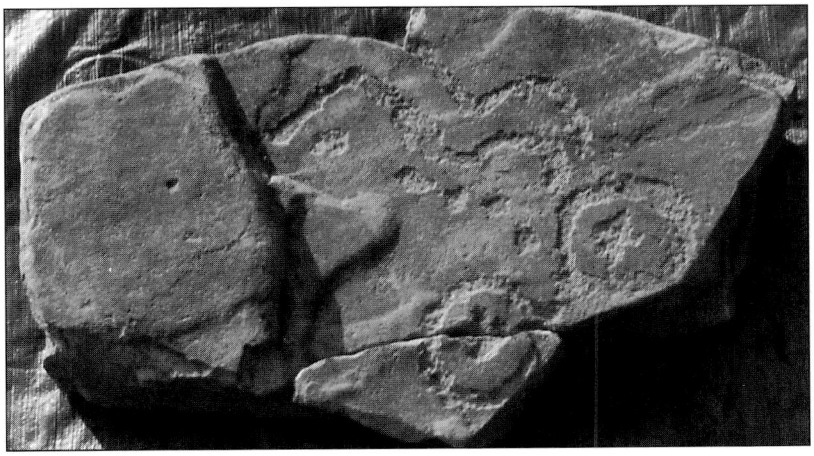

Two sides of a marked boulder in the cist

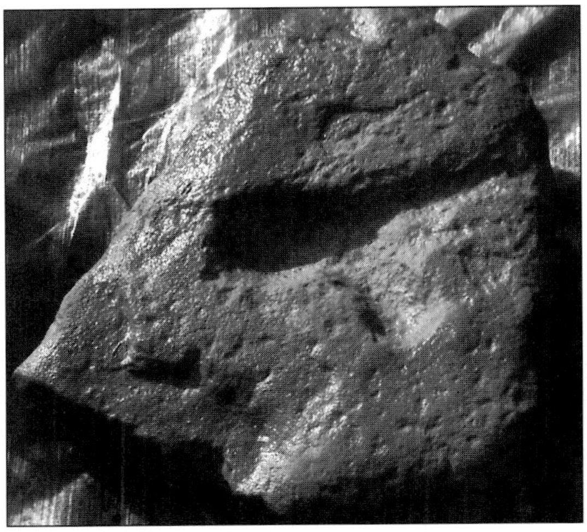

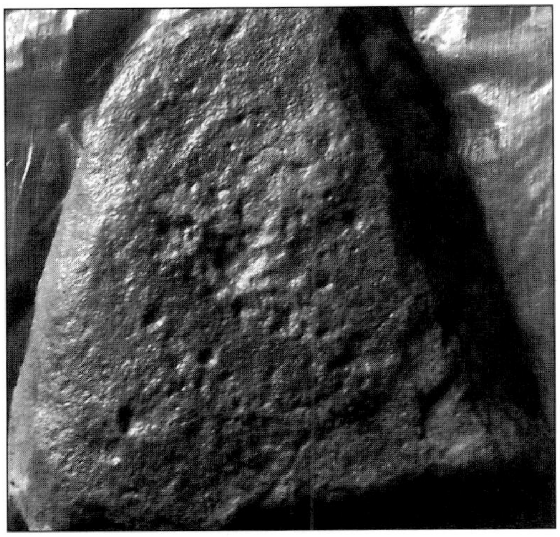

deposits. It is today as fresh as the day it was made. When it was dragged out in 1995, parts of it were broken off, but most fragments have been recovered and planned on to the drawing. The top side, which was vulnerable to plough-scarring, was covered with plain cups, two sets of which are joined by a short groove. At the 1996 summer exhibition in Durham, the cist cover lay between the Lilburn stone and the Gainford cist cover. The latter shares double-sided motifs, with contrasting simple and complex designs. The former, with its horned and other spirals, had accompanied multiple cremations in a pit. If only these finds had been made today, we should know a great deal more about the significance of rock art in prehistoric burials.

The oval pit may not be directly connected in time or function with the cist, but it had a funerary/ritual function. The plano-convex knife lying at the very base of the pit is only the eighth of its type found in all burials in Cumbria, Northumberland and Durham (another was found in the How Tallon cairn overlooking Barningham Moor). Three were associated with food vessels and urns, which makes a late Neolithic/early Bronze Age date likely for this one.

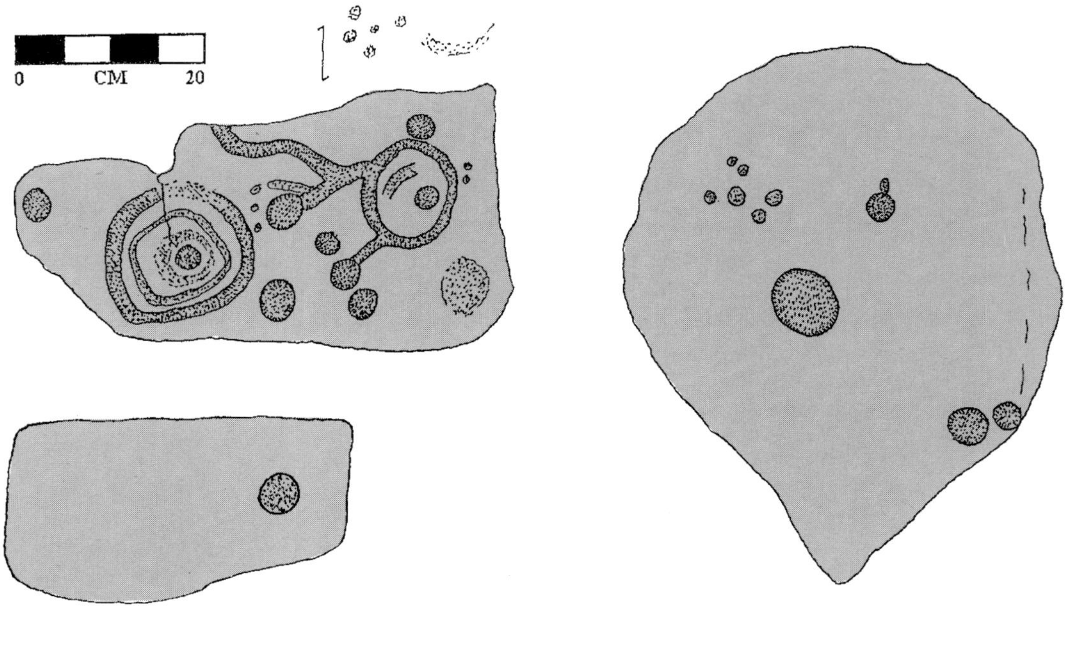

Portables from Aske Moor (Silver Hill)

# 7. Teesdale

## (i) Aske Moor, High Hag Moor, Feldom, Gayles Moor and Crumma/Dousgill

Most of the recorded rock art in this area was discovered by Stuart Feather, and there have been some additions to his work.

**Aske Moor(Silver Hill NZ139 039)**
A prominent mound, unexplored, has a wall running over it, on which are two large boulders, illustrated here. The more elaborate, with multiple concentric rings and cups, was found by Tim Laurie. The link between burial mounds and decorated cobbles, boulders and slabs is discussed in the last chapter of this book.

At NZ 1780 0406 there is a ploughed-down round barrow with a stone that has a well-defined cup mark.

**High Hag Moor**
At High Hag Moor there are three rocks with motifs, illustrated here, at an assembly point for army training. The site lies on the Whashton Green - Marske minor road near a lay-by on Sturdy House Lane, south of Sturdy House. A hard track runs parallel to a fence, behind which is a new plantation. The most interesting rock lies under a wire fence that now encloses a small area ploughed for tree planting. Near to a small car park in this new enclosure, P. Brown discovered a cup marked rock on which artificial cups have been added to natural ones, and some chert and flint flakes. This reminds us that the existence of a natural feature on a rock such as a cup/depression may have given interest in it as potential for further work, provided its position was suitable. On this site there are open views in some directions, and restricted views in others. Between 1969-79 Stuart Feather reported 6 marked rocks in this area. We have recorded only three, so others must be covered up. His first report was of one rock with three cups and three cup and ring marked stones, on War Department (now Ministry of Defence), land, in two groups. He then added "two further cup and ring marked rocks covered up by vegetation" in these two groups.

**Low Feldom Farm (NZ112 035)**
In 1981 S.Feather reported a marked rock near Low Feldom Farm. We have found two at the site, which is south of the farm in a low hollow within the steep ravine below the farm, with views down the steep Clapgate Beck. This is well sheltered, with a steep rise to the north, and in the scooped-out hollow there are several enclosures of different periods, the latest being a stone walled one with remnants of a thorn hedge on it. The rock art is not on outcrop, but on two boulders built into the walls of an earlier enclosure. Although the marks are faint, the pattern revealed by rubbings is clear.

The larger boulder lies on the north slope, and is covered with cups and connected grooves. The smaller is embedded in a rubble and earth wall, with some of its lower cups possibly continuing under the soil. The association of rock art with enclosures is a common theme, and this enclosure site also has prominent viewpoints, even though it is not at the highest point in the landscape. There are springs nearby, and the site is good for herding and hunting. The third slab (NZ 1045 0460) had fallen off a wall, and is now at the Bowes Museum. The farm is uninhabited, like so much else in this area, and access is not encouraged as it is part of the Feldom military ranges, and can be dangerous. The Range Warden must always be contacted should anyone wish to visit the site.

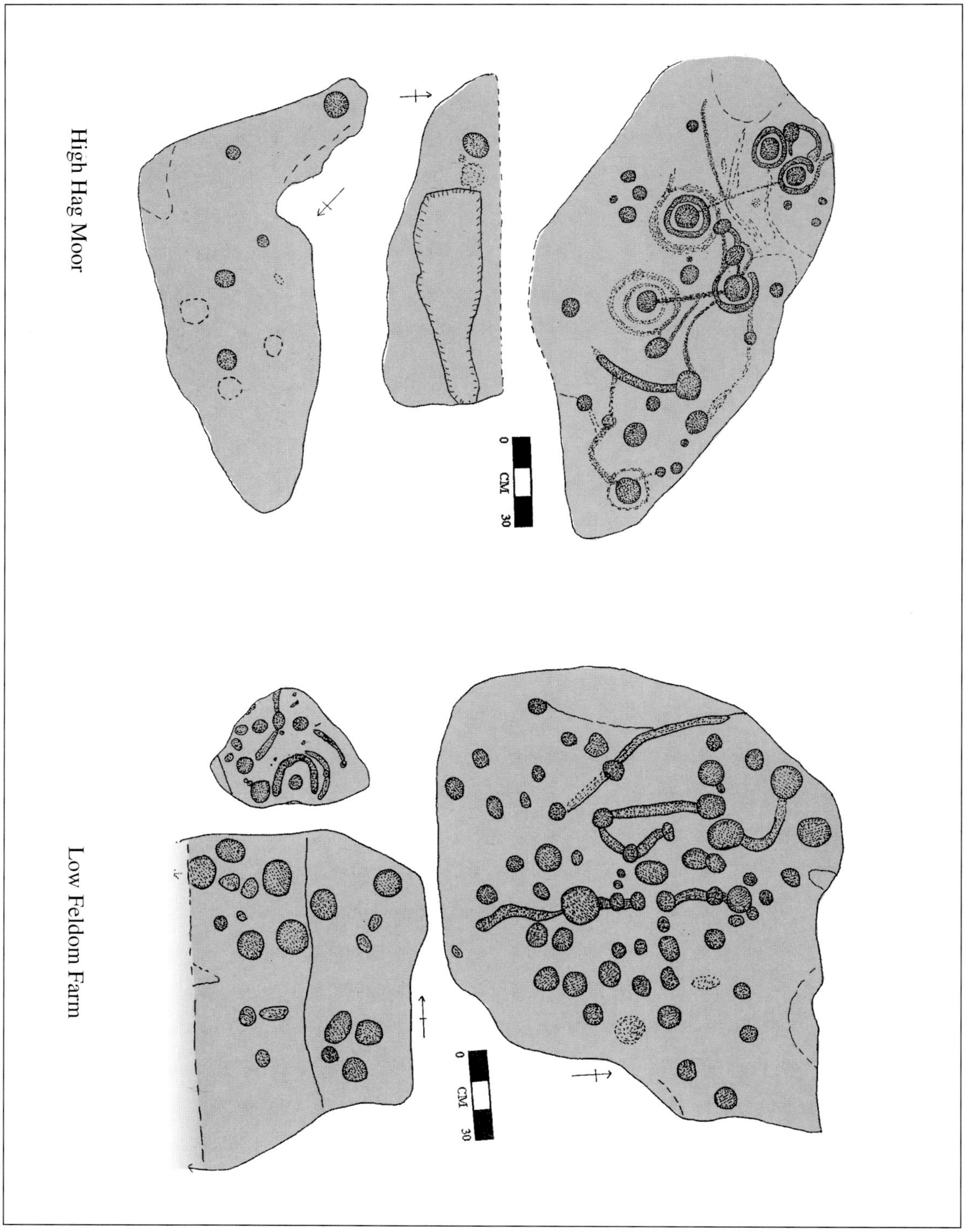
High Hag Moor
0 CM 30
Low Feldom Farm
0 CM 30

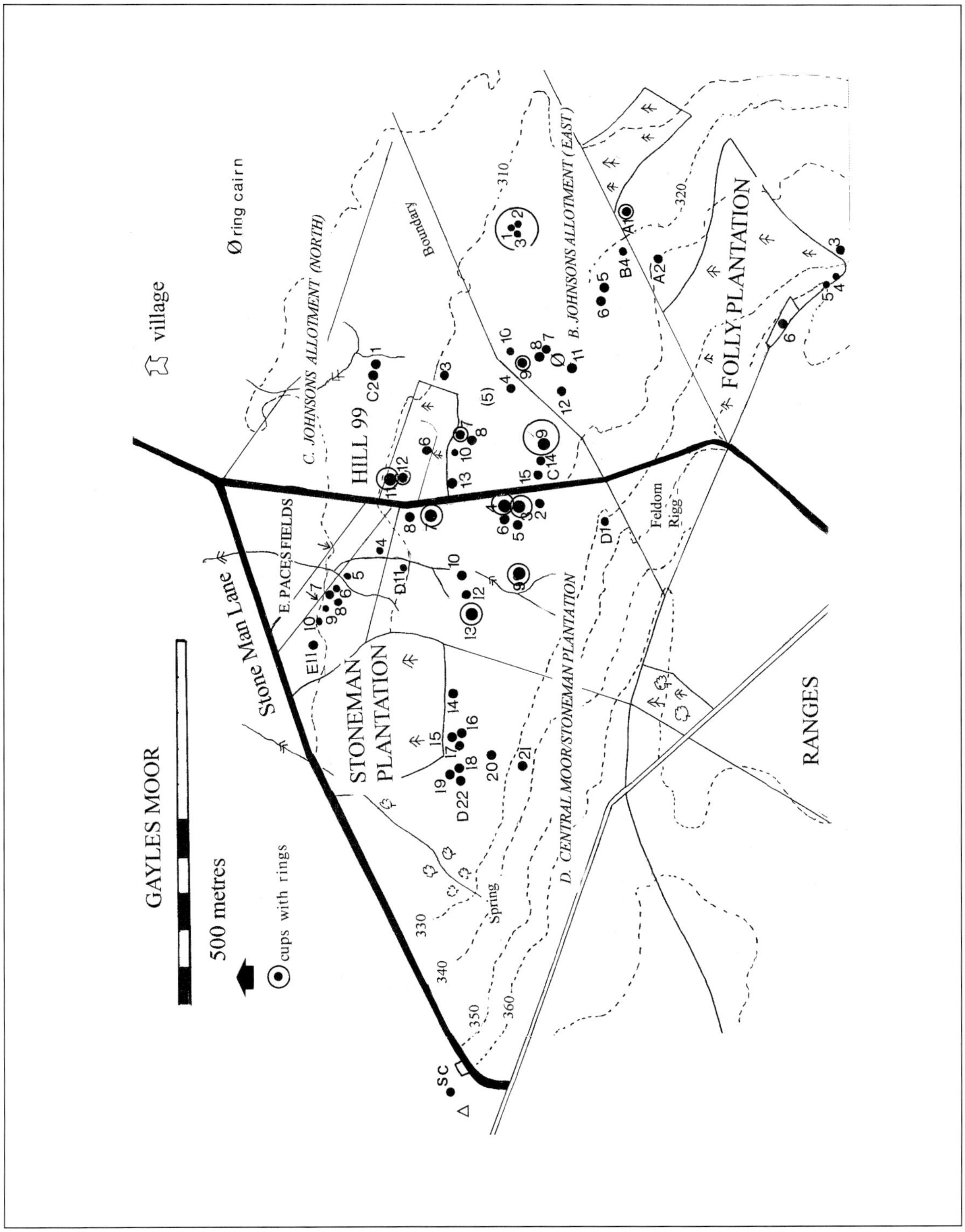
GAYLES MOOR
500 metres
cups with rings
ring cairn
village
Stone Man Lane
E. PACES FIELDS
STONEMAN PLANTATION
HILL 99
C. JOHNSONS ALLOTMENT (NORTH)
Boundary
B. JOHNSONS ALLOTMENT (EAST)
FOLLY PLANTATION
D. CENTRAL MOOR/STONEMAN PLANTATION
Feldom Rigg
RANGES
Spring
SC
310
320
330
340
350
360

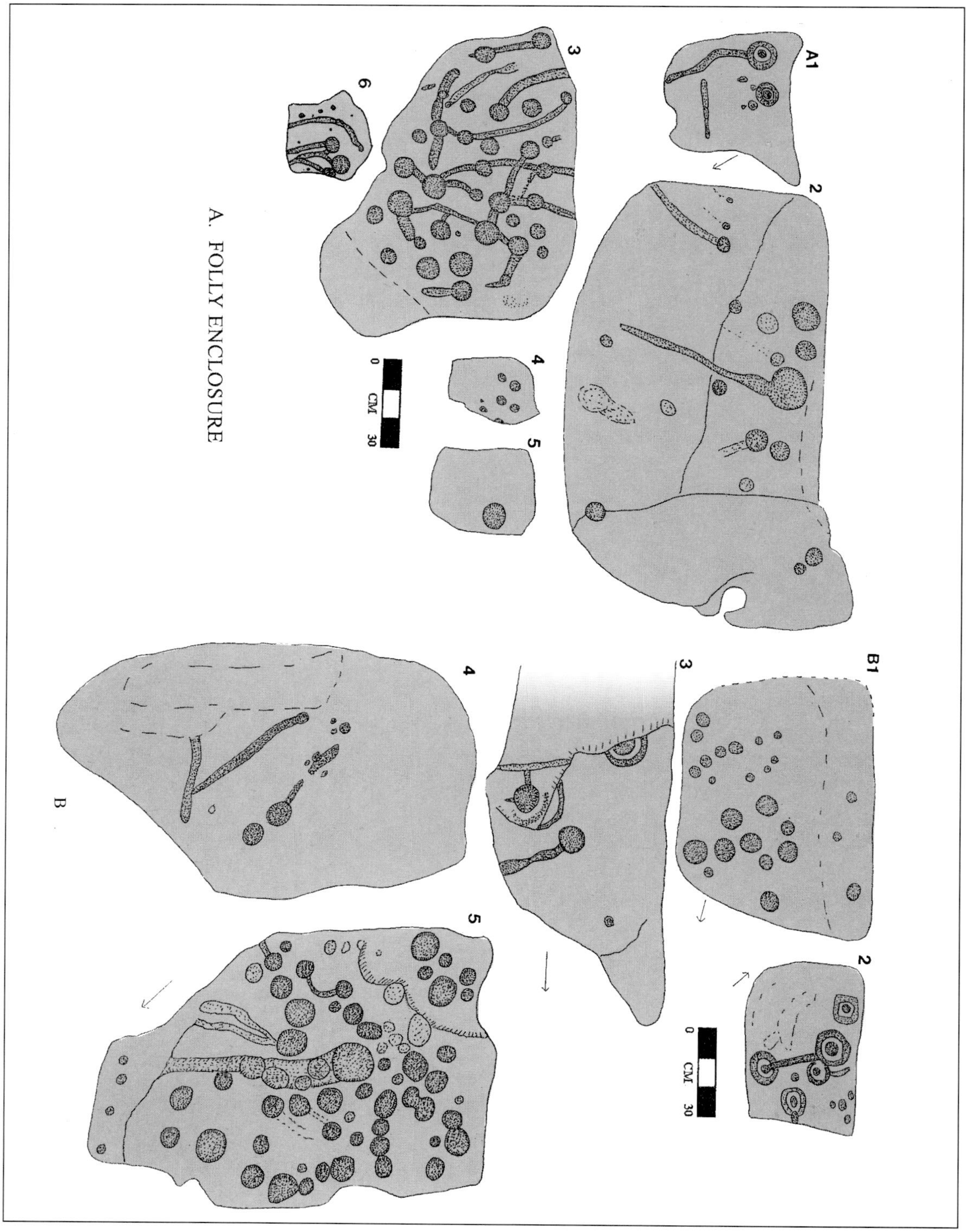
A. FOLLY ENCLOSURE
A1
2
3
4
5
6
0 CM 30
B
B1
2
3
4
5
0 CM 30

## Gayles Moor

On Gayles Moor is an open linear group of marked rocks extending east-west on an elevated terrace of gently-sloping moorland, about 2,000m long and 1,000m wide. All rocks are above 350m OD., their southern boundary being the ridge of Feldom and Folly Plantation.

The rock markings focus on Hill 99, a prominent large tumulus-like mound that is probably of glacial origin, though its use as a burial mound is possible. There are scatters of earthfast slabs and boulders, many half-buried in heather and marsh grass.

Most of this area is given over to rough grazing and to heather moorland. It is used by the army as a training ground. There are a few isolated trees, some planted areas, minor quarries, modern walling, faint signs of early low field walls and small cairns. To the far west is Stoneman Cairn, with a nearby marked boulder, and Dousgill (Crumma), with three marked rocks. For convenience, we have divided the area into 5 zones, in which the rocks are generally numbered from east to west.

The initial discovery of these sites belongs to Jack Blackburn, of Dalton village, who reported C9 to his brother-in-law, Mr.C. Stafford, who lives in Bradford. Stuart Feather brought his class up to the moor (Mr. Stafford being a member), in the 1960s, and discovered more rock art, hut sites, cairns and flints. These discoveries were mapped, but not published, and we were able to re-examine the map in 1996, thanks to Mr.Blackburn and Paul Brown. Tim Laurie recorded most of the rocks, and these were plotted by Defence Land Services G.P.S. They are now scheduled monuments, and for the first time each rock has been accurately drawn. Paul Brown has liaised closely with Mr.Stafford and helped to bring all the lost rocks to our notice, as well as discovering some new ones.

### a. Folly Enclosure

The northern limit of this modern enclosure is marked by a modern drystone wall. South of the wall is an interesting area with a scooped-out valley with mound deposits on a fairly even floor, and with its flanking ridge to the SW it forms a natural enclosure. It marks the watershed. Coarse, thin grass predominates, with the remains of some small trees, and a scatter of stone. One small horizontal earthfast (1) has cups, rings and grooves, and lies on the enclosure floor.

On the ridge side, with a view over the natural enclosure and the southern part of Gayles Moor towards the Tees valley, is a marked rounded block of sandstone with a vertical face (2). The top and two sides are cup marked. The motifs appear to emphasise the importance of this sheltered coomb. No 3 is in an unusual location; it lies in a small valley between two linear hills (glacial) just above the place where a spring emerges.
4 and 5 are small cupped stones in a wall, and 6 may well have come from a wall; it was found among stones used to make a campfire, but fortunately was not burnt. It is now at the Bowes Museum. Normally stones are left in situ, but not if they are in danger.

### b. Johnson's Allotment(East)

This is a roughly rectangular modern enclosure bounded by two drystone walls and the road. The first cluster of rocks (1-3) lies on a fairly level piece of ground that ends with a wall before plunging to the valley to the ENE. The viewpoints are considerable, including Hill 99, the whole of the Rigg and Folly Plantation. There is little surface stone in the immediate area.

1 is cupped, 2 cup and ringed, but 3 is special. It is one of the most important rocks because it has been quarried in prehistoric times as well as more recently. The top left cup and ring have been cut in half. Another faintly pecked arc has been cut

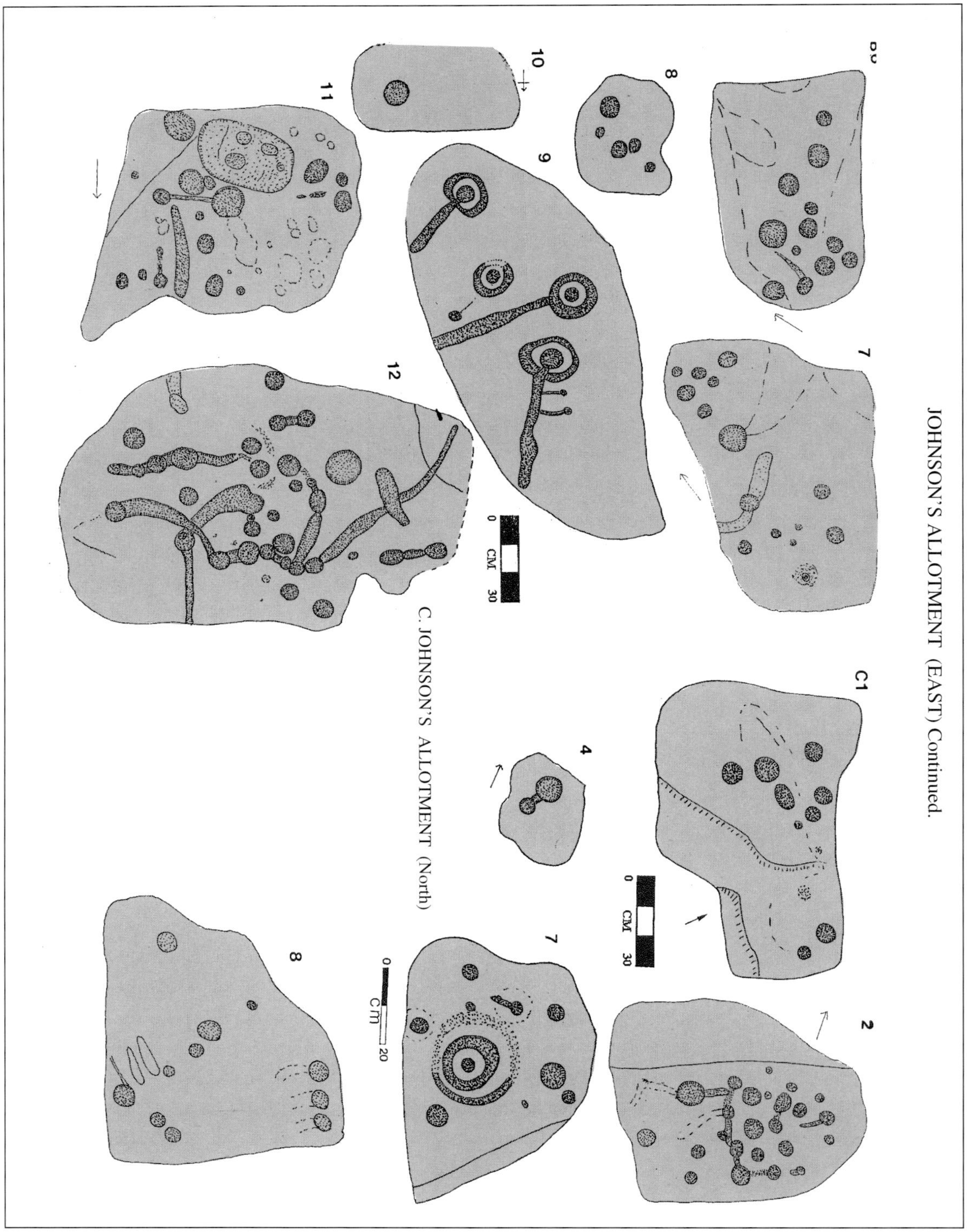
JOHNSON'S ALLOTMENT (EAST) Continued.
8
10
11
9
7
12
0 CM 30
C. JOHNSON'S ALLOTMENT (North)
C1
4
0 CM 30
7
2
0 cm 20
8

through, a piece removed, and a new 4cm deep cup and groove have been added at the new lower level. New pecking is evident along the removed edges. This is a rare example, noted on two sites in Northumberland, of the removal in prehistoric times of decorated rock (for transfer to a monument?) and the 're-sanctification' of that rock.

The rest of the marked rocks are further west, and several rocks are west of a small knoll on which a ring cairn has been built. Some stand clear of swampy ground, some are almost lost in heather, and others are embedded in old enclosure banks. 12 lies in such a bank, a boulder with motifs that are predominantly a series of grooves made of cups, like beads on a string. No.5 is similar. Although cups predominate, No.9 has rings included in the design, like No.2.

**c. Johnson's Allotment (North)**

This area includes Hill 99 and North Gill Head. To look first at the general picture: a spread of marked rocks, some in groups, occupies a shelf of land 320-330m high, in a line, gently sloping to the north. This includes those on Johnson's Allotment (East). The rocks are difficult to see because few are naturally outstanding, and vegetation easily obscures them. It is the wide views from the rocks that is so striking, and not the observer's view of their position. There is little stone scatter in this area; minor quarrying and possible field clearance for small enclosures only account for superficial removal. It is unlikely that the thin soils would have supported much arable, if any. No rigg and furrow is evident. Its use today, apart from the military, is rough pasture for sheep: coarse grass and heather.

The most northerly stones in the area (1and 2) are on a ridge overlooking a small stream valley and springs. 3 is a single cupped stone east of Hill 99 wood, 4 has two linked cups near the south boundary wall, 5 is embedded in a low boundary wall and now grown over since it was photographed. Stone 6 is a large, disturbed slab with a single cup in the wood. 7, 8, and 10 lie just south of the wood.

In the Enclosure there are two rocks that are more elaborate. To the north of Hill 99 and visible over the wire fence and gate that enclose the plantation over this huge mound, is a large block of fell sandstone, a survivor of a quarried rock aligned roughly N-S(11). It has a design of cups and rings sometimes known as a 'keyhole' pattern, unique here, and very rare in England and Scotland. It helps to distinguish the mound area from the rest of the moor, and we know that other marked rocks may be buried as a result of tree planting and military activity. One survivor is a slab on the east slope of the mound (12), with its cups and faint rings. Stone 9, a flat slab, has one of the finest examples of rock art, as the drawing and photograph show, and there are signs that part has been quarried off. Between it and the road are two almost hidden rocks (14 and 15) with cups and grooves.

All the above rocks lie to the east of the narrow tarmac road that leads to Gayles village. The areas that follow all lie to the west of that road, which provides access to a good representative selection of rock art without your having to stray too far from the road, an important consideration in a military area.

**d. Central Moor/Stoneman Plantation**

This area extends from the road to the western limit of the rock art on this moor. A few coniferous trees mark the remains of woodland, and Stoneman Plantation is new woodland. To the north, the area ends with a wire fence. Most of the marked rocks to the west are cupped boulders and blocks. In the west, the land falls to a small stream. Rocks 18, 19 and 22 are close to small cairns or ring cairns. The eastern moor, near the road, includes some very fine complex markings. Stone 1 is a cupped earthfast block, the highest in

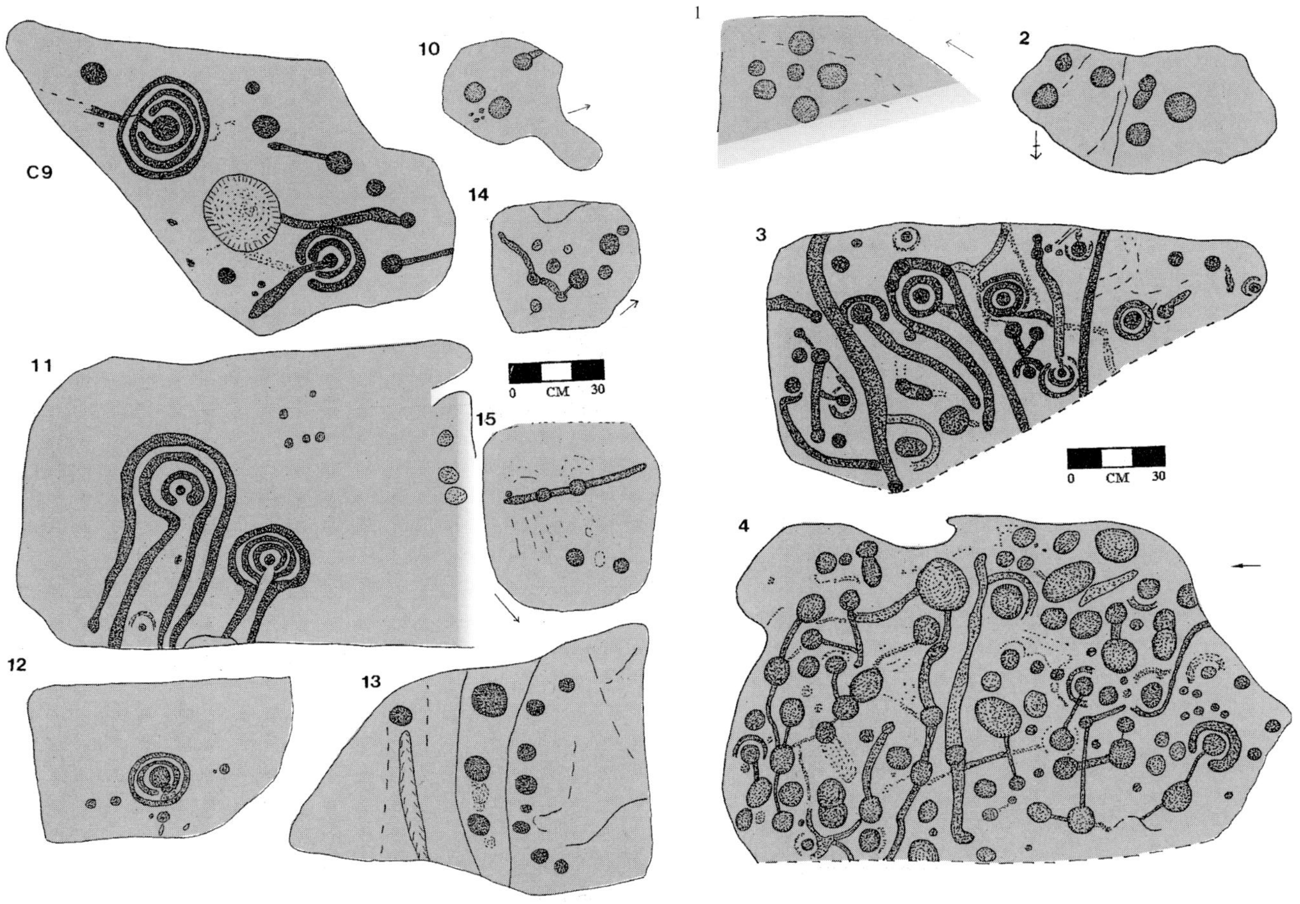


C. Johnson's Allotment (North)

D. Central Moor

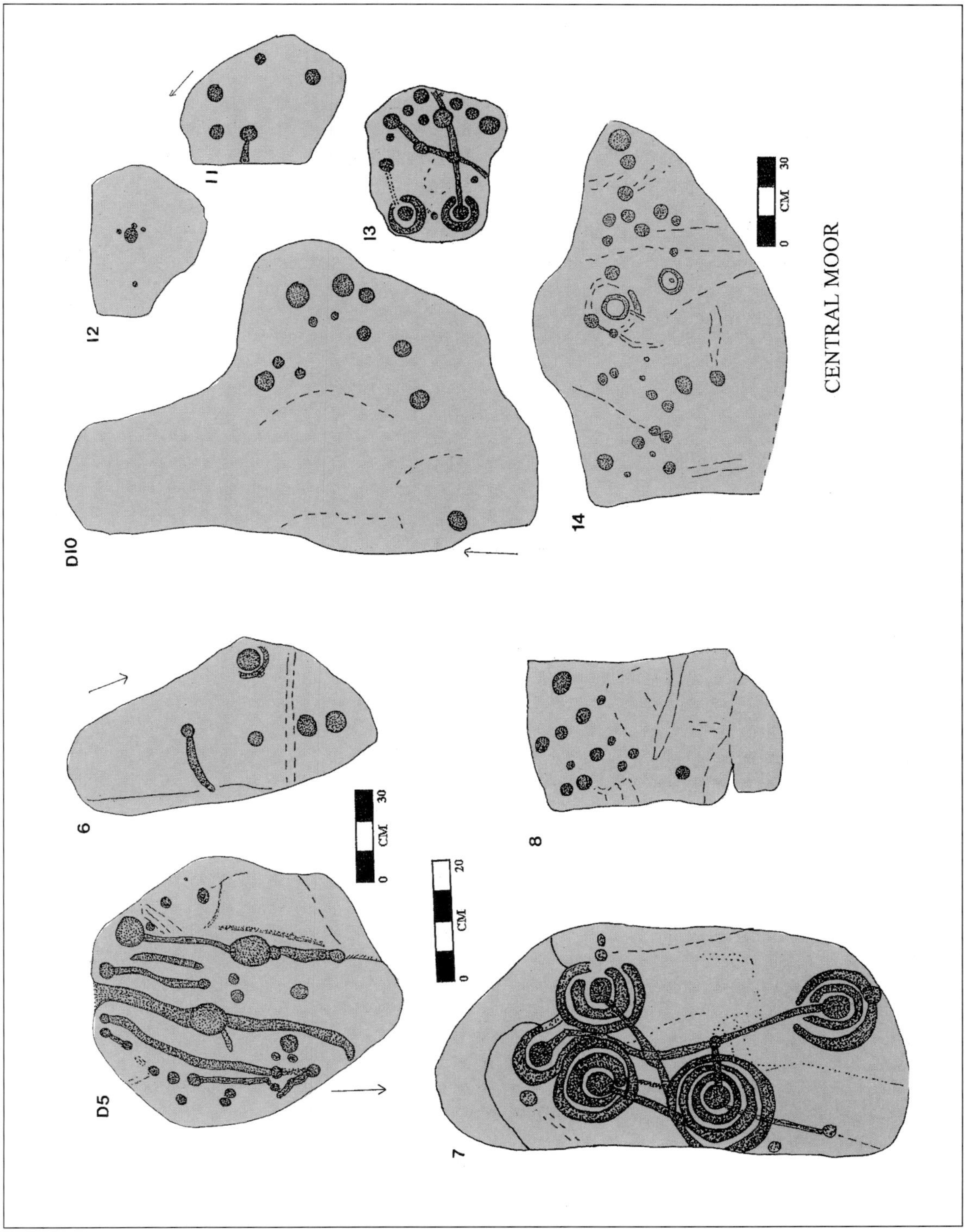

D5
6
7
8
D10
11
12
13
14
0 CM 30
0 CM 20
CENTRAL MOOR

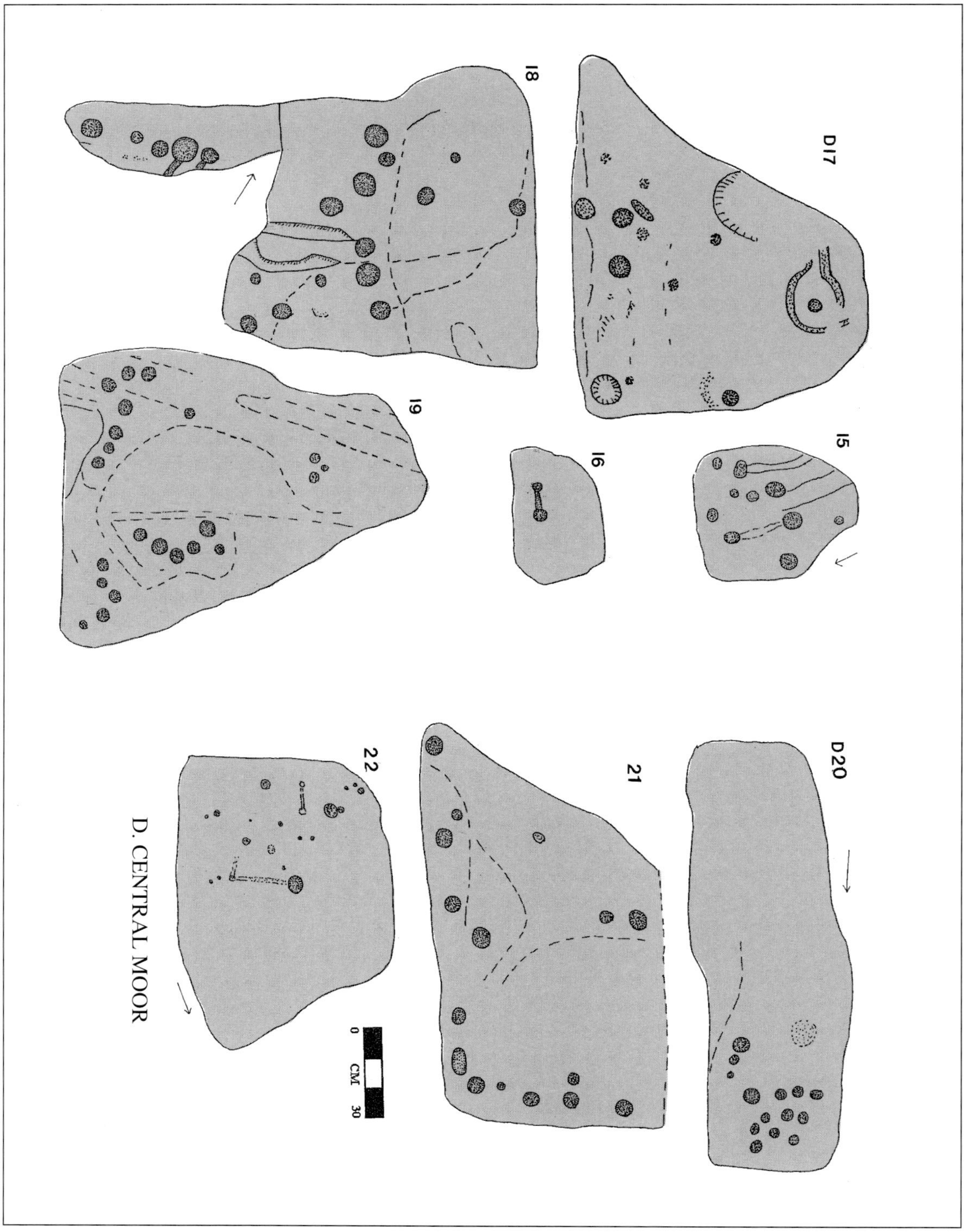
18
D17
19
16
15
D20
21
22
0 CM 30
D. CENTRAL MOOR

this area, that overlooks a ring cairn over the whole moor to the valley. Stone 2 is a recently found cupped block that has been partly quarried away, and leads to two of the most decorated blocks, 3 and 4. No. 5 is a rounded boulder that has cups and cups linked by grooves. 6 is a slab with 5 cups, one with a groove and one with a partial ring. Further north, 7 is a flat slab 16m west of the road, and its complex motifs are packed on to a relatively small surface. Stone 8 contrasts with its near neighbour, with simple cups. Back to the south, 9 is known as the 'rosette' stone, and has already been described in detail. It lies beside the early course of a small stream. 10 is a slab, 11 and 12 are small rocks, and although 13 is a small slab, it has cups, rings and grooves that form an interesting design.

The other stones lie to the west of a wire fence. 14 is 15m from the wood, and is a tilted slab with cups and two faint rings. 4m south of it is 15, a small boulder with two joined cups. 16 is an upstanding boulder with cups and groove 25m. south of the wood, on the edge of a knoll above a small stream to the west. 17 is a rounded boulder partly obscured by heather, with cups, and some natural grooves. The illustrations show the rest to be cupped, with 18 a block of earthfast, 19 about 25m south of it, 20 with its cup cluster on a pillow-shaped boulder, and 21 on the higher ground, a large quarried earthfast block with most of its cups on two edges. The furthest west, 22 , is a flat slab with a cup and faint signs of the beginnings of others. It is 16m. from 19, after which the land rises, then falls away to the west.

**e. Paces Fields**

Named after a demolished house, this is furthest north, marked off from the rest by a wire fence, and including dry stone walls which were found to include rocks with motifs that presumably had been quarried from earthfasts. The numbering system begins with these wall stones, then continues from east to west. Some were discovered by Stuart Feather's group, and the rest by Paul Brown. 1-3 are the wall stones, the last still in position in the wall as a through stone. 4 is a single cup marked embedded boulder (not drawn). 5 holds a dominant place, a large block with markings on two levels. 6 is a very odd arrangement: it seems that the centre has been taken out, and one part of it was found lying on the wall. The cups are very well made, and some are linked. The illustrations of the others (7-11) speak for themselves. The last stone in this area is much further to the NW, at Stoneman Cairn. The stone lies close to it, an upstanding boulder with cups and grooves, with very wide views from it, one of the best viewpoints in the area. Stoneman, incidentally, means the stone mound.

**Crumma/Dousgill**

Although three important marked rocks lie on the farm belonging to Dousgill, the easiest access point is through a gate into a field opposite the track that leads to Crumma House. Permission must be obtained to view these rocks. The inset map shows the square that corresponds with the 09-10 easting and the 07-08 northing. The site is at c.320m, the land sloping to the Dous Gill on the north, with higher ground to the NW.

The field gate opens onto a track that passes between two small quarry scoops. There is a linear glacial mound to the right (NE), at the foot of which is a scatter of rocks, one of which is marked with grooves that are formed by joining cups that are deeply set into the rock. To the left (NW), in a square fenced-off enclosure at the edge of a thin plantation, is a flat slab with a curved groove, and over the wall in rough pasture overlooking Dousgill Farm is a pillow-sized boulder below a mound, covered on one face with deep cups, some joined. The three rocks all lie below mounds, and there is in the same area a distinct circular, prominent mound. There is no certainty that the marked rocks are in their original positions. From all the marked rocks are wide views except to the west and SW, where the land is higher.

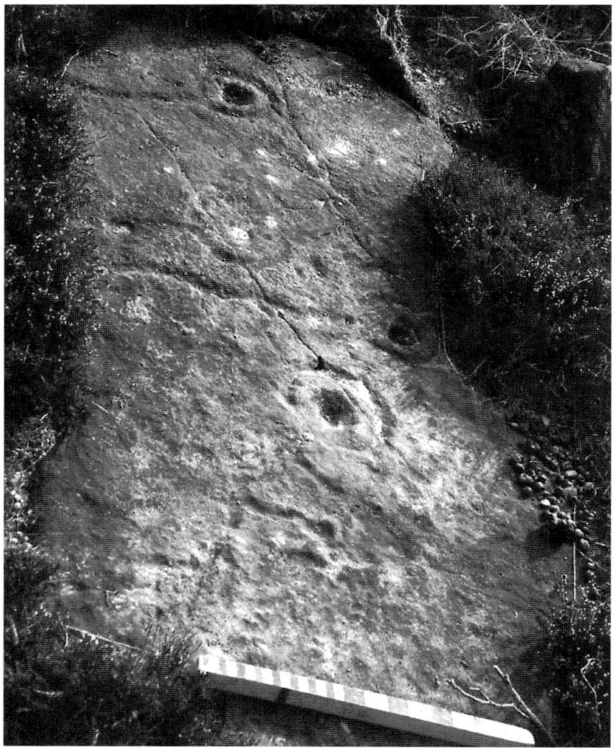

*Most of these sites lie on military ranges, and access is limited. There are many warning signs, and red flags fly when firing takes place. Generally, the Gayles Moor sites are open to the public on Sunday afternoons and Mondays, but this is not always the case. The Range Warden needs to be contacted before one considers a visit.*

GAYLES MOOR, B9 and D3

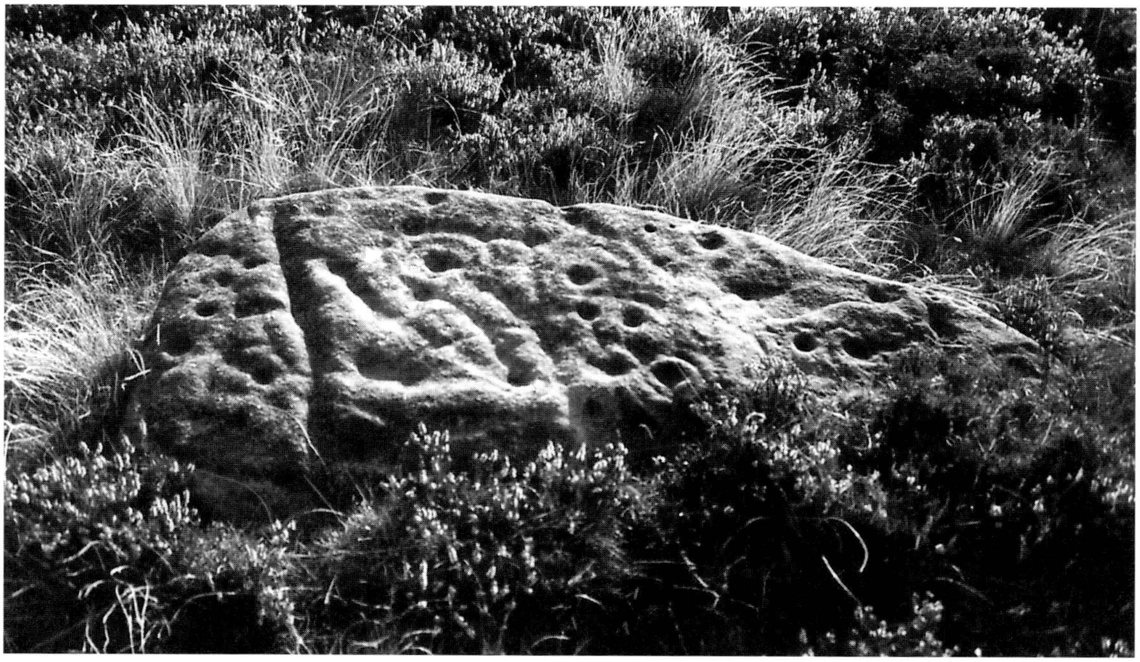

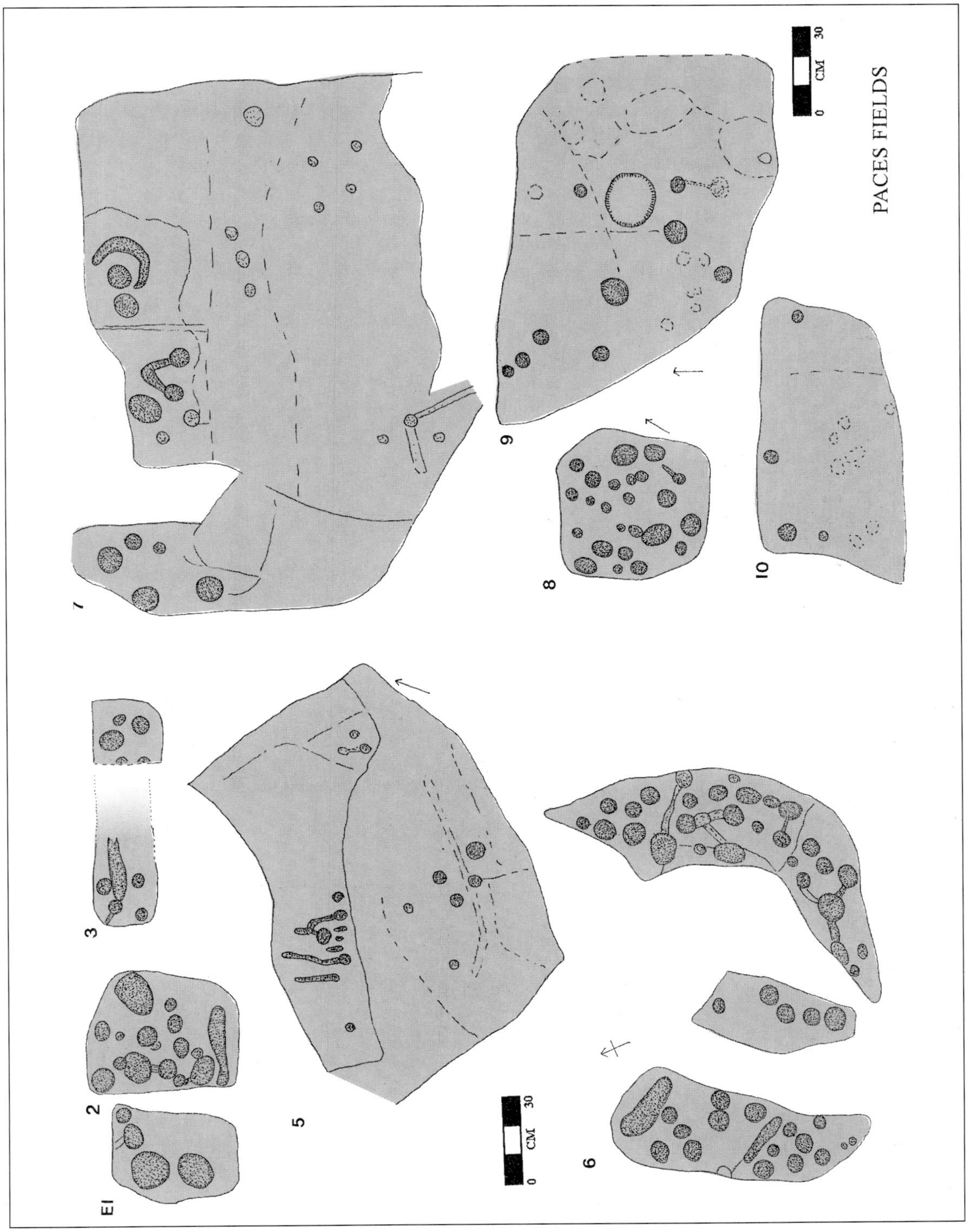
PACES FIELDS
0 CM 30
E1
2
3
5
6
7
8
9
10

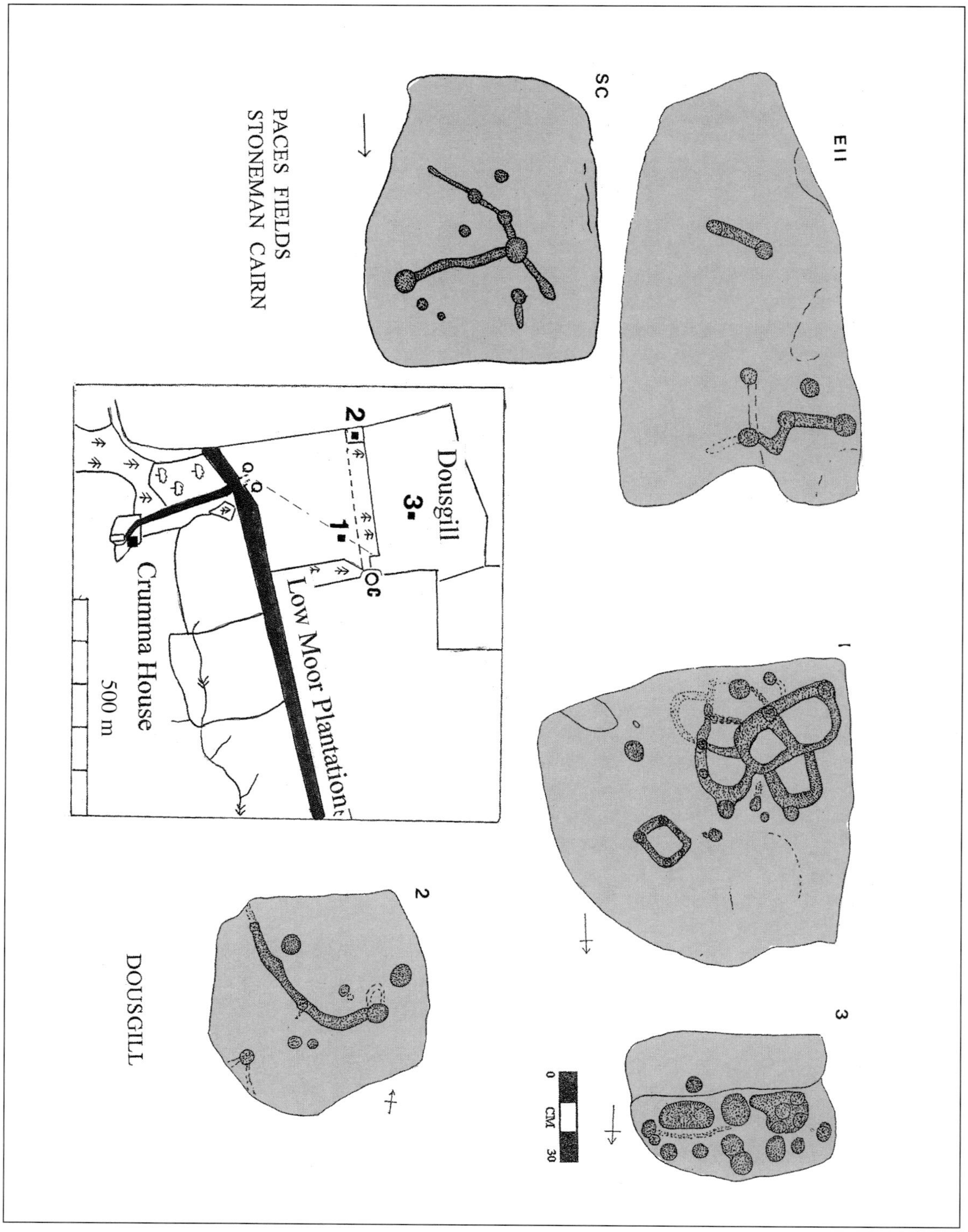
SC
E11
PACES FIELDS
STONEMAN CAIRN
Dousgill
3
2
1
OC
Low Moor Plantation
Crumma House
500 m
1
2
3
DOUSGILL
0
CM
30

C5 lodged in a low boundary wall.

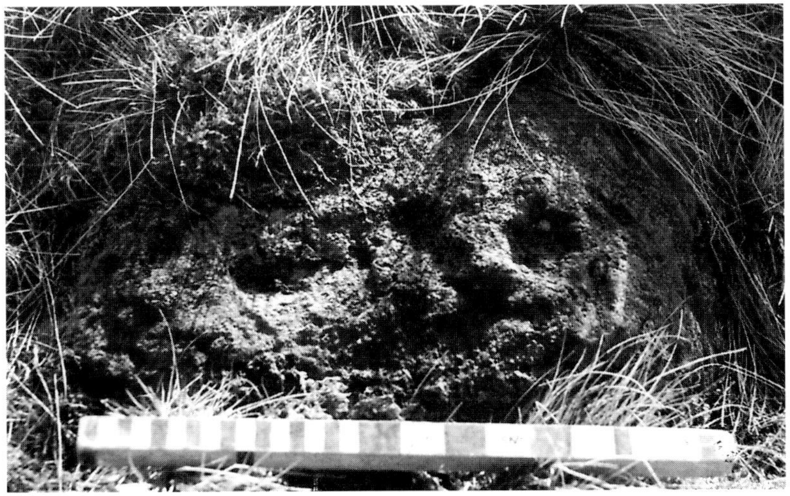

D7

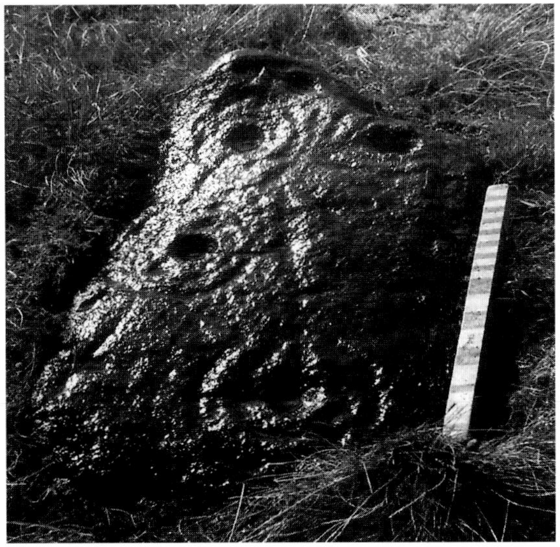

Dousgill 1.

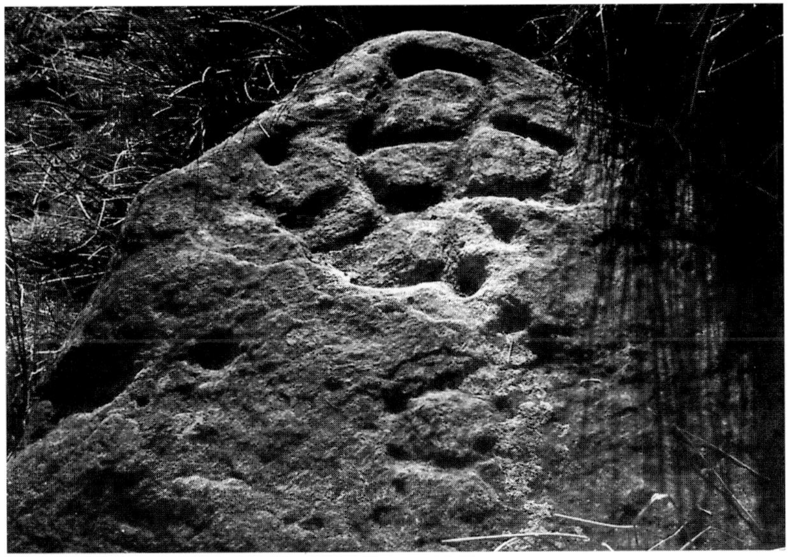

D13

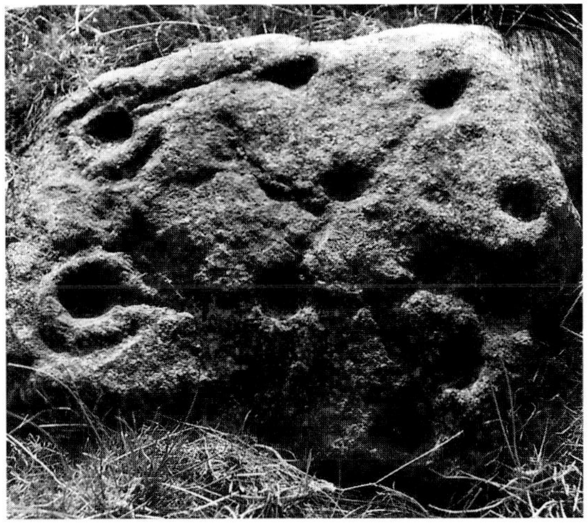

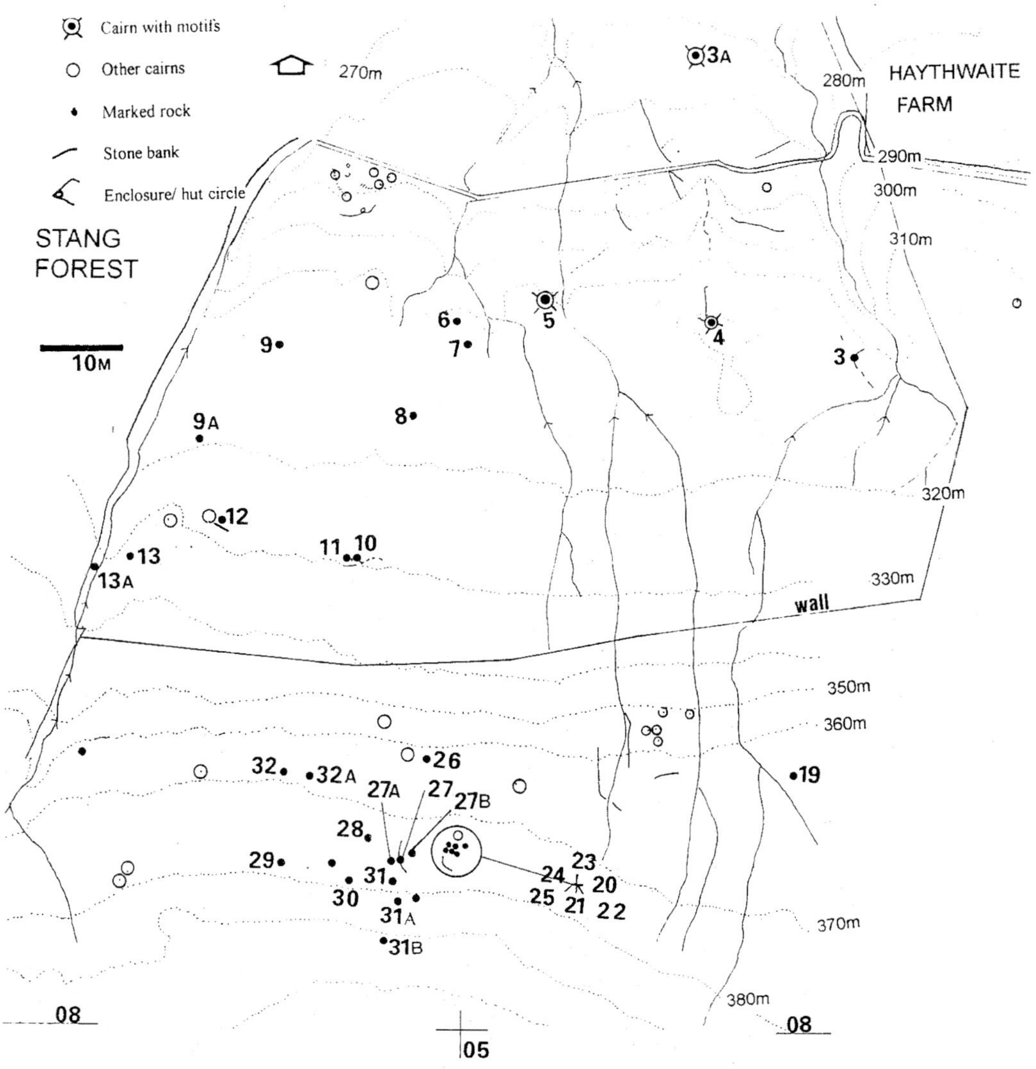


BARNINGHAM MOOR WEST AND SOUTH-WEST AREAS

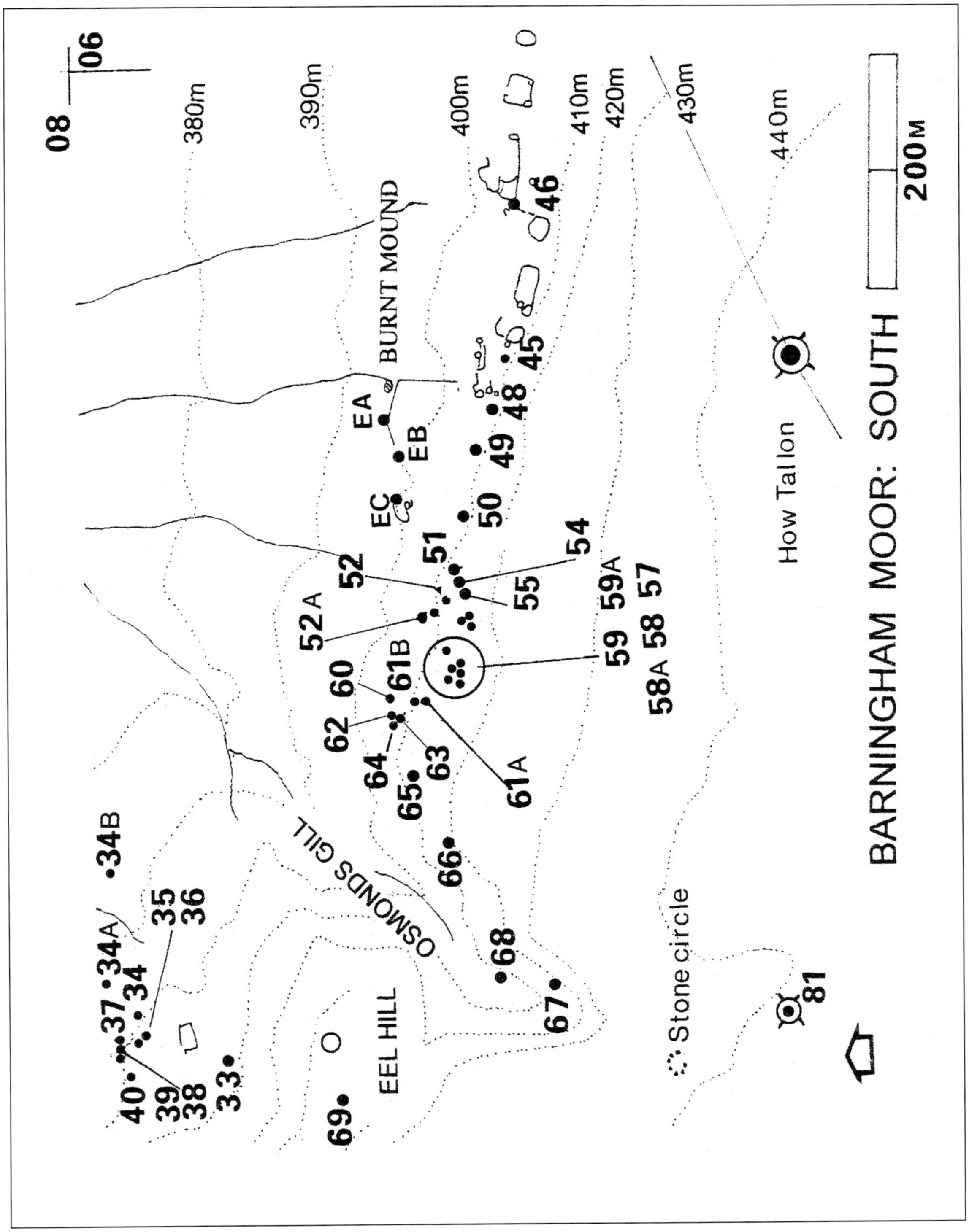

BARNINGHAM MOOR: SOUTH
08
06
380m
390m
400m
410m
420m
430m
440m
200M
BURNT MOUND
EA
EB
EC
How Tallon
Stone circle
OSMONDS GILL
EEL HILL
33
34
34A
34B
35
36
37
38
39
40
45
46
48
49
50
51
52
52A
54
55
57
58
58A
59
59A
60
61A
61B
62
63
64
65
66
67
68
69
81

## (ii) Barningham Moor

Barningham Moor is within Barningham Estate, owned by Sir Anthony Milbank, Bart. It is a grouse preserve and an important conservation area for ground-nesting birds during spring and early summer, when disturbance is not advised. Public rights of way provide access to How Tallon, a round barrow with marked rocks, and a view point at Grid Reference NZ 0575 0745, OS trig. point 447m.(1467') OD. The Badger Way, a very ancient trackway, one of many green tracks over the Pennines, crosses the Moor and provides an alternative high level access to the Moor from the Newsham-Holgate road. (Park at either Byers Hill or near Long Green Farm).

This account has two parts: (1) a background to the geology and general archaeology of the area, and (2) a complete survey of all the rock art. The bibliography refers readers to further information.

### An overall view:

Barningham Low Moor extends south from the enclosed pastures of the farms of Bragg House, Moorcock and Haythwaite which lie to the north and below the unenclosed road from Barningham village to Stang Foot through to East and West Hope in the Stang Forest. The Low Moor is mainly covered with heather with some rough sedge and grass pasture. Above, and to the west of Haythwaite Farm, it rises gently towards the How Tallon ridge and Eel Hill. Small streamlets rise as springs near Osmonds Gill below quarried fell sandstone and limestone strata which outcrop to form a low but steep final scarp edge before the How Tallon ridge is reached. These small streams have been controlled to flow through a leat which crosses Washbeck Green and the low Moor to provide an earlier water supply to Barningham village and Park. Other springs and streams rise from the slopes below Eel Hill and within Haythwaite Allotment, the large rough pasture enclosed by a modern wall which includes Scale Knoll.

Scale Knoll and West Langbrough are lateral moraine ridges formed by the Stainmore Glacier, an ice stream which was fed from distant snow fields above the eastern flanks of The Lake District, bringing with it erratic boulders of Shap granite, deposited in the Greta and lower Tees valley. Several granite boulders can be found on the slopes below Eel Hill. Motifs have not been found on the granite, probably because it was too hard for stone tools. The Stainmore ice also deposited a scatter of local fell sandstone slabs and blocks over the surface of the moor and embedded them earthfast into the glacial boulder clay which covers the shale, sandstone and limestone bedrock. These strata outcrop to form a steep scarp edge below How Tallon and Eel Hill, and have been heavily quarried.

The scarp is cut by Osmonds Gill (Osmaril on the OS.map), a strange, deep, dry valley that has no surface water except for the powerful spring that rises at the lower entrance to the gill. Although there is no stream, the sound of water is heard in the gill after heavy rain. Together with the Cross Gill behind Eel Hill, it was formed by sub glacial streams from and below the southern edge of the Stainmore ice. Rocks with markings more elaborate than simple cups favour the vicinity of springs and streams rising from Osmonds Gill and the northern slopes of Eel Hill. They cluster near Osmonds Gill, Washbeck Green and Scale Knoll.

Some marked rocks are associated with round barrows, notably with the excavated How Tallon. At the top of Osmonds Gill is a circle of 7 surviving sandstone blocks, which should be considered together with rock art and round barrows in a late Neolithic or early Bronze Age landscape on the southern edge of Teesdale, where access from the Tees to the Swale across the watershed would be convenient. The south-facing slopes of the How Tallon ridge favoured Middle Stone Age occupation above Arndale Springs. Scatters of flint and chert implements of the Neolithic period indicate the sites of the later hunter-pastoralist activities. Near springs below Osmonds Gill are burnt, crescentic mounds of fire-cracked and reddened sandstone cobbles. Seventy four burnt mound sites have been recognised in Wensleydale, Swaledale and Teesdale. One, above Holwick Head in upper Teesdale, is made entirely of reddened fire cracked stone, and in his excavation, Denis Coggins has confirmed charcoal inside it, a fragment of polished stone axe and flints, possibly Neolithic (Coggins,D. pers.comm.). These mounds are oval, circular or crescentic, made of burnt sandstone or whinstone, and a single site has 1-3 mounds arranged around a central or peripheral depression, likely to be a trough in which water was brought to boil by heated stones pushed down from hearths on the mounds themselves. Their size depends on the frequency of use. All are situated on the brim of small streams, often within 50m of the spring head or rise, always on open ground with wide views. All but one are above 300m OD. In Ireland more than 2,000 such mounds are known. Recently in Northumberland two out of four at Titlington have been excavated, and were of Early Bronze Age origins. In Ireland some give dates up to the 5th Century AD. The Irish sites indicate what they were used for. Hearths and pits lined with clay, stone or planks were recorded. The amount of stone indicates the frequency of use. Boiling in a pit, and roasting in stone-lined ovens are recorded, and it has been demonstrated that 100 gallons of water can be brought to boil in a wooden trough in half an hour. Stake holes of oval or circular huts nearby are recorded. It seems that burnt mounds are for an activity not associated with permanent occupation any more than a shooting hut, which is used now for a maximum of 12 days for grouse and partridge-driving . They can be considered as picnic saunas, alfresco dilettante-group-feasting places with wild boar on the menu, and saunas where flagellants apply birch branches after hot baths in steaming tents! Après hunt, in fact. The two sites on Barningham Moor have only recently been recognised, so this brief description of their general significance in a larger area helps us to see their possible use here.

Indistinct curvilinear (sub-circular) enclosures and field banks of stone-dump construction, with small stone-dump cairns or clearance heaps are found at Washbeck Green and below Eel Hill. Such sites are consistent with the earliest farming community settlements. A fine example, a prominent linear settlement of stone walled enclosures with circular and rectangular huts or buildings can be found on the terrace below How Tallon and by analogy probably dates to the late prehistoric Iron Age or Roman period. Stone-founded settlements often succeed earlier timber settlements which leave no surface trace. At least one of the 'hut circles' below How Tallon may be a small Bronze Age ring cairn. The settlement has five separate enclosures on a terrace that is permanently shaded from the low sun by the north-facing scarp above it. There are clearly worn trackways that enter from the east and west that are distant from any recent farm or settlement and do not lead to quarries or lead mines. They suggest the movement of cattle. The marked rocks on the same terrace are residual and earlier than the stone settlement.

## The Marked Rock Surfaces

All the decorated rocks are drawn, but this section is to give sufficient detail to place them in a sequence that could be conveniently followed, subject to prior permission, from Barningham Estate.

Begin at the west end of Barningham village, where careful verge-side parking is available near the cattle grid. Views to the west over the Greta valley towards Stainmore and Mickle Fell, to the north across the lower Tees valley and to the east across the south Durham lowlands to the coast are unrestricted on a clear day. Views south are more restricted by ridges. We cannot assume that the marked rocks were always on open moorland. Pollen analysis shows that it was not until about 600BC (approximately) that the moors became open, with heather, sedges and grasses dominant. Before that, the Pennine uplands were wooded, and only the thin calcareous soils over outcrop limestone would have been open, and the high moors, with birch and alder, would have been more or less open. So rock art would have been within a wooded setting, and only those rocks in the first clearance pastures, or on the highest slopes overlooking the tops of woodland trees, would have had unrestricted views of the kind we see today.

By good fortune, our survey of prehistoric sites has been mutually advantageous to English Heritage in their survey of 1997, for our sharing of information has led to the discovery of more marked rocks than we began with. We are grateful for their allowing us to adjust our maps accordingly. Any rocks added to our survey recently appear with the suffix A and B, and any additional discoveries can be similarly incorporated into our numbering system without altering the whole thing. A westward extension of our sites into and through the relatively modern obstacle of The Stang Plantation is inevitable, as cup marked rocks have now been found at Scargill. They are listed as Stang Foot, SF1-3, No.1 being at NZ 0270 0978.

**Barningham Moor (Rocks 1-2)**

The numbering system in this section puts No.1 (NZ 0755 0995) as the most northerly and easterly. It is an unobtrusive earthfast rock, slightly sloping, with cups and grooves that follow the downward slope as the design elements, from it one can see the whole of the Greta valley to the north, and a large stretch of the moorland. In contrast, No.2 is a block of sandstone incorporated within a close setting of three similar large blocks to form a structure open to the north. This cup-marked setting of rocks is a few metres south of an embanked curvilinear enclosure, originally revetted with large rocks, Grey Stones. This site may be interpreted as either an embanked stone circle similar to those in Derbyshire and the North York Moors, or a later prehistoric settlement. Approximately 150m west of Grey Stones, on the west bank of the stream are two hut circles with an adjacent circular embanked 'yard'. One of the hut circles is cut by drainage ditches of the road. A saddle quern and polished whinstone top rubber stone were found where these ditches cut through. To the south-west is a cairn and a cup marked stone at Rowley Intake, found in 1997.

**Sites in the allotment west of Haythwaite Farm (Rocks 3-13A)**

The continuation of the northern ridge, just south of Haythwaite Farm and the narrow tarmac road, marks the northern limit of the marked rocks, on the line of the Scale Knoll hills, broken up by streams that rise gently to the south and cut through the ridge on their way north to join the Gill Beck and the Greta. Stone 3A was found during an English Heritage survey in 1997, and lies on lower ground to the north on a cairn. The hills have some rock art (4,5) on two cairns, and No.3 is positioned as part of a stone alignment that ends with the steep valley of the Scales Knoll Beck to the east. The view from 3 is down the stream valley, and the other viewpoints look mainly south across the area of rough pasture enclosed by a modern wall that forms a rectangle around it, before the land rises again to the south.

At first glance the land seems fairly uniform, but

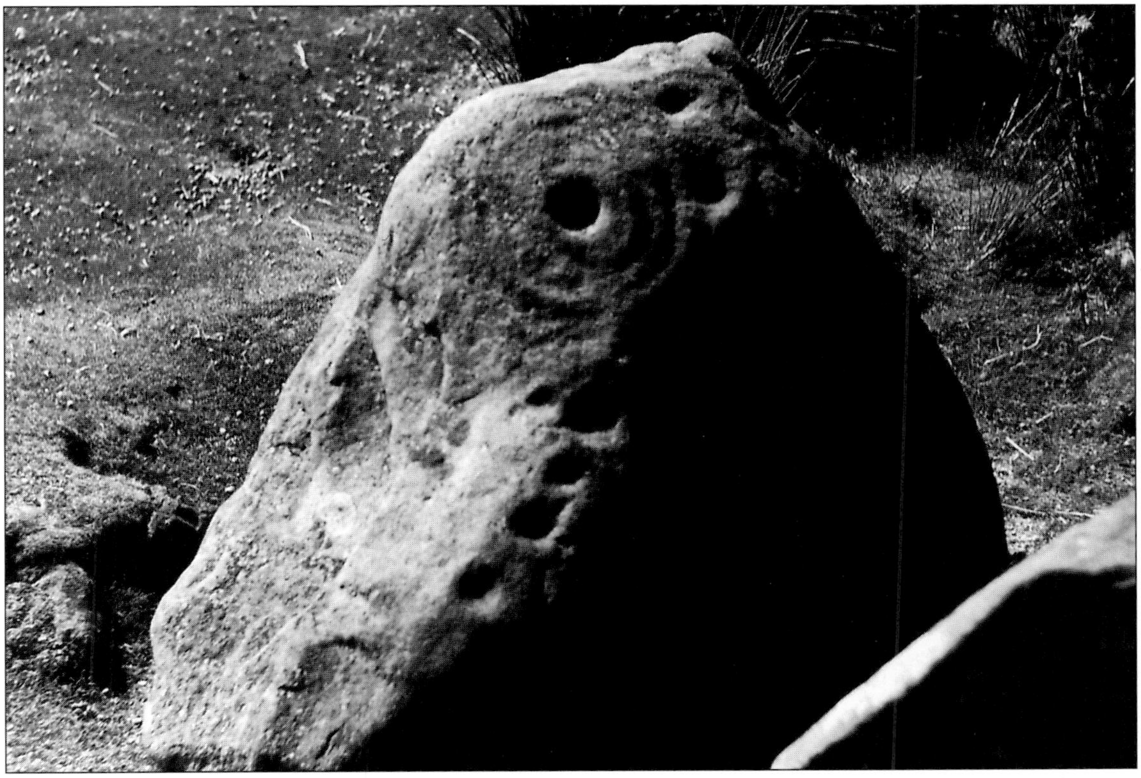

Barningham 3, and its setting, looking North

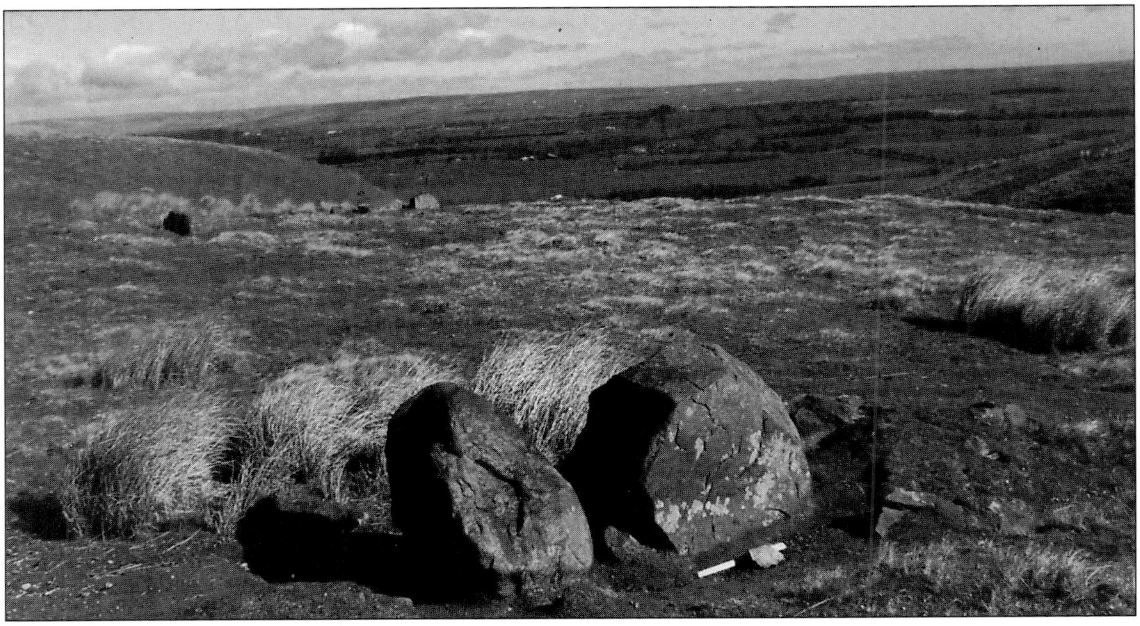

closer acquantance shows it to be broken up in marshy tracts of streams flowing from south to north. Small knolls that lie above the marsh make the crossing of this area easier. These higher parts are where the rock art is located.

There is a cluster of three small marked rocks (6,7,8) on one of the knolls, overlooked by cairns on Scale Knoll itself, two of which have a double and a single ring in their composition. No.6 is an example of the art form packing in as much as possible on a small, triangular-shaped earthfast, where cups and rings jostle each other for position and grooves run down the slope into the ground. The top is much eroded, the lower part best preserved, but all can be seen in brightly oblique light. It is high and visible, which makes the siting of 7 something of a mystery. 7 lies on the east slope of the knoll (in thick bracken) above a stream and lay undiscovered until August 1996 because the visible sides were unmarked. The vertical west face is marked, and has subsequently become buried. No.8 is flat with the grass-covered ground, and from it there is a wide sweep of vision, whereas the views from 6 are restricted by the knoll. These rises in the ground, however slight, were significant. The locations chosen are usually the best viewpoints with enough suitable stone for marking, and a position high enough to clear the marshy ground. 9 is flush with the grass on a bare, rounded hill east of the Stang Forest, surrounded by marsh, SW towards the next rise is 9A, and from these rocks Haythwaite Farm, and the whole of the enclosure to the south and the ridges beyond are visible .

So far no rock art has been found in the east-west centre band of the walled enclosure, probably because it was marshy. the next cluster is to the SW, where the land rises slightly and where there are traces of ancient walled enclosures. Although rocks 10-12 lie close to these enclosures, they cannot be associated with these early fields. On the ridge overlooking the Woodclose Gill is a cairn near which, on the west slope, is a cup and grooved sloping slab (13). It used to mark the most westerly edge of rock art, defined by the stream valley between it and the Stang Forest, until Paul Brown found the largest marked slab on the moor in 1997 (13A). The motifs are remarkable, as they incorporate rectilinear patterns, and because the pick marking is completely fresh. Indeed, this is a perfect example of how the markings were made, using a stone chisel about 1cm at its end. The block, often obscured by bracken, lies at the foot of the wall on the west of the burn, The views from all these rocks are extensive in many directions.

**The Central Area (Rocks 14-19)**

This area contains some of the rare multiple concentric circle designs, and they are within a fairly narrow linear band.

Stone14 is a small vertical slab with cups on top, close to a streamlet. 15 is a large flat slab covered with cups, crowded by a stone heap. To the north there is an extensive view to the Greta valley over a large expanse of coarse grass , and patches of grass and heather. To the south are uninterrupted views to Osmonds Gill (at 220°) and to a shed on the hillside below How Tallon (at 172°). 14 is 43m away (at 120°). Close by is a distinct enclosure, and within it is a difficult to find block among heather clumps; it has a complex design that incorporates multiple penannulars around cups with grooves leading out, and an almost rectangular groove around cup clusters. Roughly west of this, WNW of the grouse butts, is 17, an isolated slab east of the track to Haythwaite Farm where the grouse butts form a line, and this is at a considerable viewpoint. However, like the others, it would have been difficult to find unless you knew what you were looking for. 17A, with cups and grooves, was found further north during the 1997 survey. The track beside the grouse butts south also follows a stream valley, and at grouse

**The How Tallon Ridge Burial Cairns (70-82)**

The last group of motifs in this section, further south, makes an interesting link between burial cairns and rock motifs. Whereas it is valid to suggest that marked rocks were uprooted to provide building material for cairns, it is equally valid to suggest that there was something special about incorporating motifs in cairns. Some marked rocks are clearly not removed outcrop or earthfasts, but are deliberately selected cobbles, some marked on more than one surface. We know that at least 8 marked rocks were incorporated in the building of the large burial mound called How Tallon. Seven are cupped, but one has elaborate designs on all faces of a cobble sandstone. Another has cups on two faces. Unfortunately, some of these important rocks have been removed and built into a wall over the cairn, and there may be more. There is a good case for demolishing the wall, removing the marked rocks to a museum, and rebuilding the wall.

How Tallon was excavated in 1897, and the finds and reports were re-examined in 1980.
There were 5 burials and a central empty cist ( a stone-lined box in a pit). There was a contracted body in a cist with fragments of a food vessel, and the remains of another body above the empty central cist with fragments of possible beaker. It is believed that the empty cist at the centre was the first burial to be made, and the others, from the pottery, would be somewhere around 2,000BC (late Neolithic/early Bronze Age). We know that the marked stones in such a cairn are purpose-made and not fortuitous field clearance. At the time of the excavation, the marked rocks were either not seen or ignored. Many have distinct pick marks visible.

There is a fine display of material from the How Tallon excavation in the Bowes Museum, and it would be good in the future to see the addition of the marked cobbles. The display also relates the amusing but sad tale of the excavation, so different in resources and intent from today's careful archaeological work. An extract from Sir Frederick Milbank's account explains all.
"I sent the men forward in the morning, and then rode up about noon to How Tallon. They had just come upon the stone of another cist. This proved quite empty when we opened it, but above it was a body, the skull of which was in perfect condition. Birtwhistle, the keeper, held it in his hands to shew it me, but while he did so the wind blew upon it, and it fell to pieces excepting the cheek bones and jaws, which were in the most perfect order".

The 13 flint implements in the mound cannot be placed in a definite context. They include broken barb-and-tang arrowheads, a plano-convex knife, earlier leaf-shaped arrow points, scrapers and other worked flints, all of which fit happily into a general late Neolithic/early Bronze Age context, as the pottery.

Other cairns at Frankinshaw How (78-80) and above the head of Osmonds Gill (81) have motifs incorporated in them, and close to the latter is a small stone circle, making this an interesting ritual centre. However, we know nothing else about the cairns, which are undisturbed and long may they remain so. Other cairns on and below Scale Knoll have cup marks thus six cairns have marked stones in their composition.

At Frankinshaw Well (82) there is a large tilted block of earthfast rock, just above the stream bed, that has large cups at the top and grooves that run down from them. Natural erosion may have caused this, but some of the grooves link other cups. All around it, there is erosion that intensifies almost daily, and this has exposed a significant flint and chert flaking site that includes a wide time-span of artefacts. It is another example of the use of a site in prehistoric times by many cultures, again close to decorated rocks.

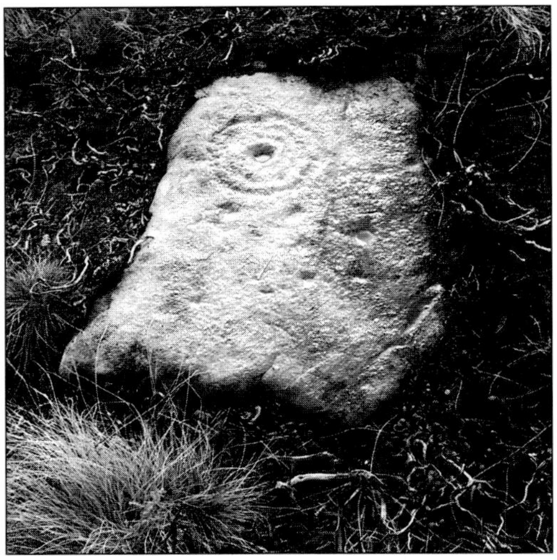

BARNINGHAM 17

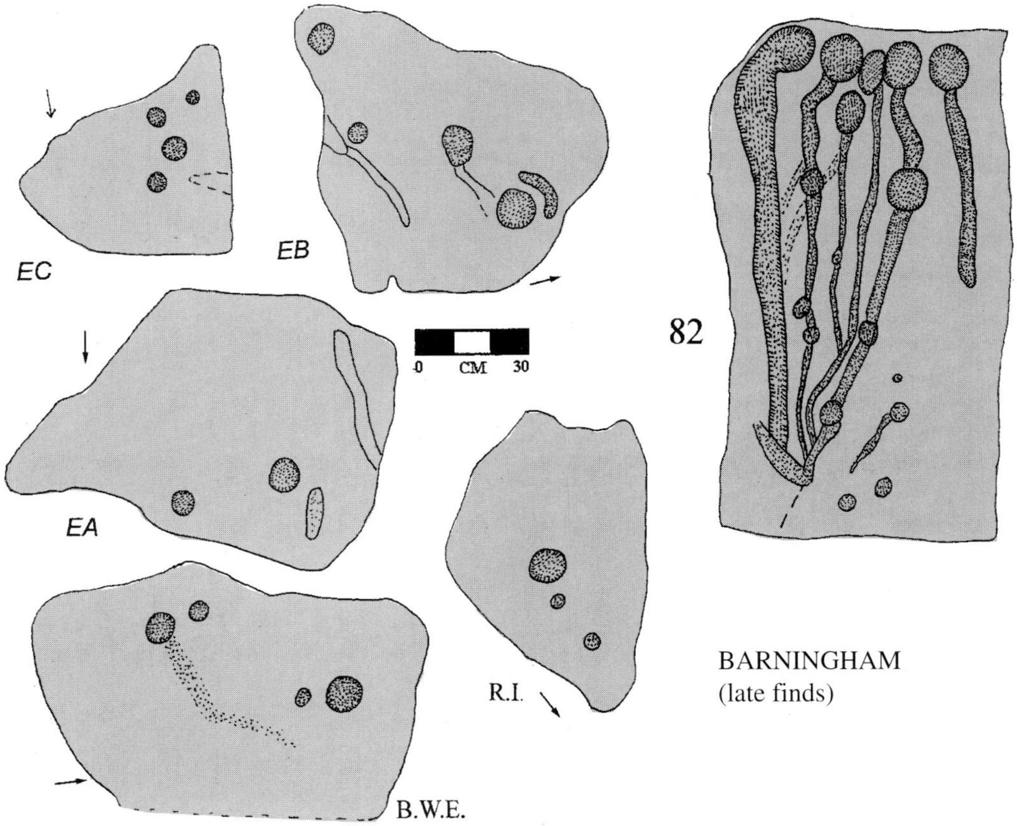


BARNINGHAM
(late finds)

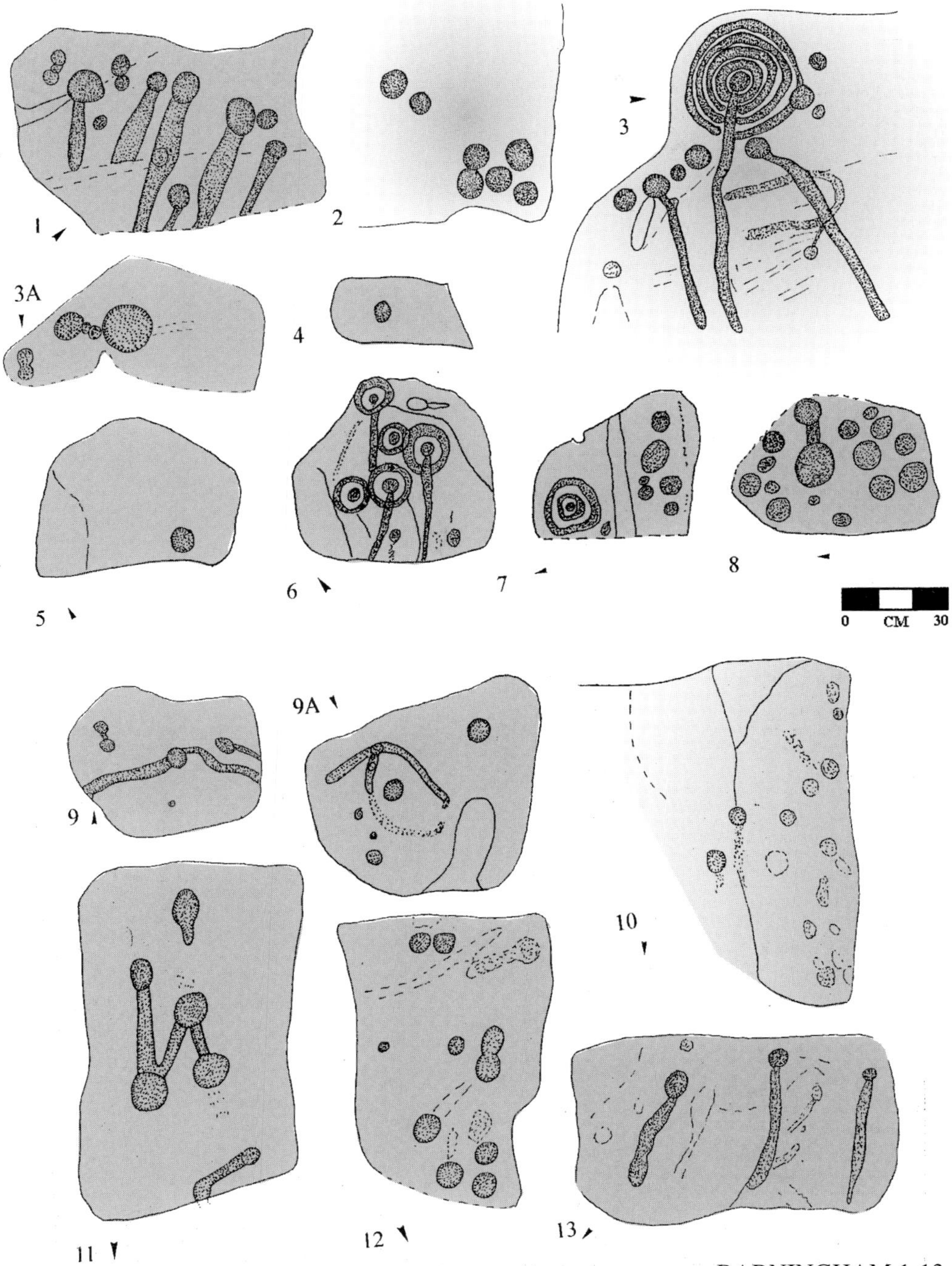


BARNINGHAM 1-13

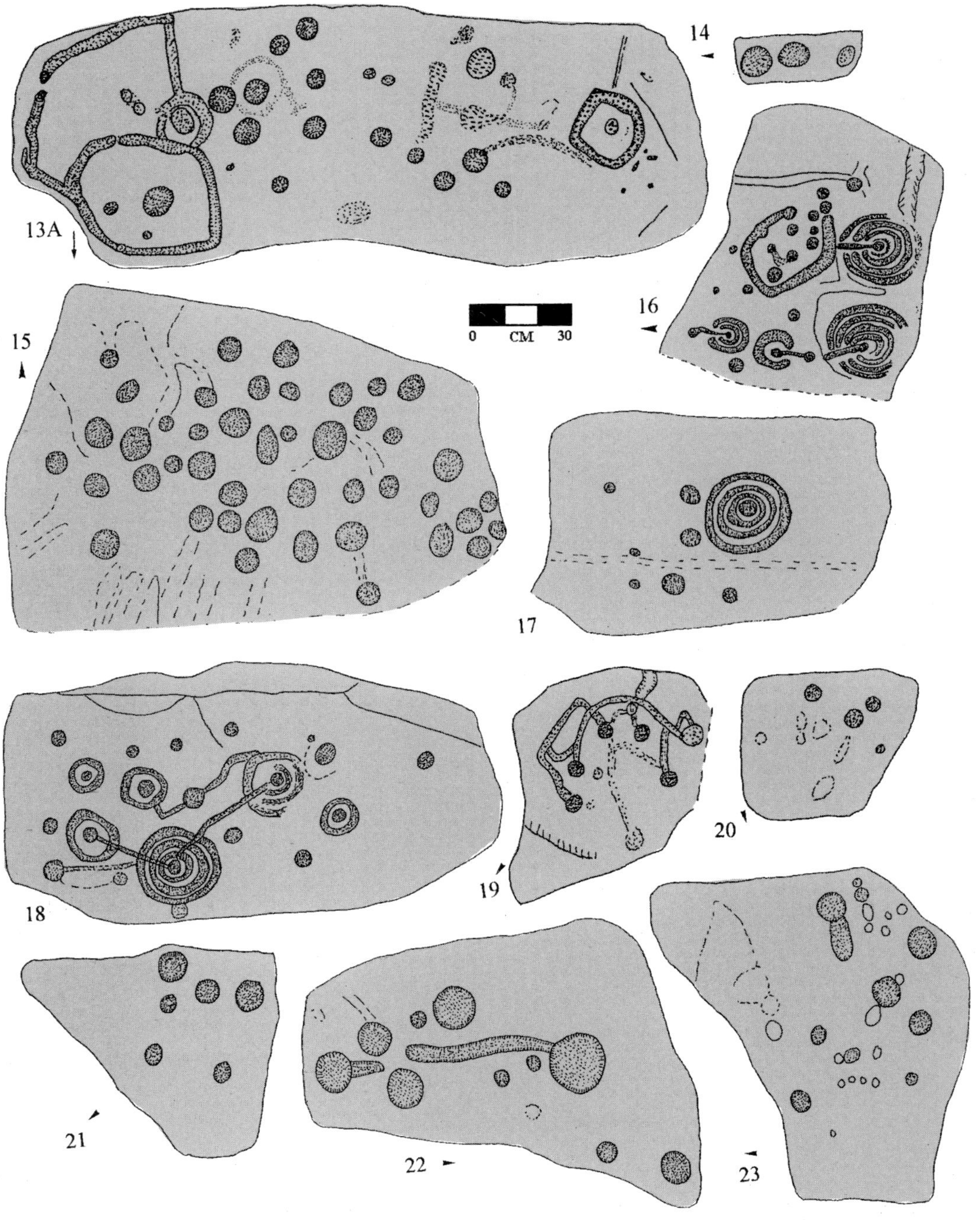

BARNINGHAM 13A - 23

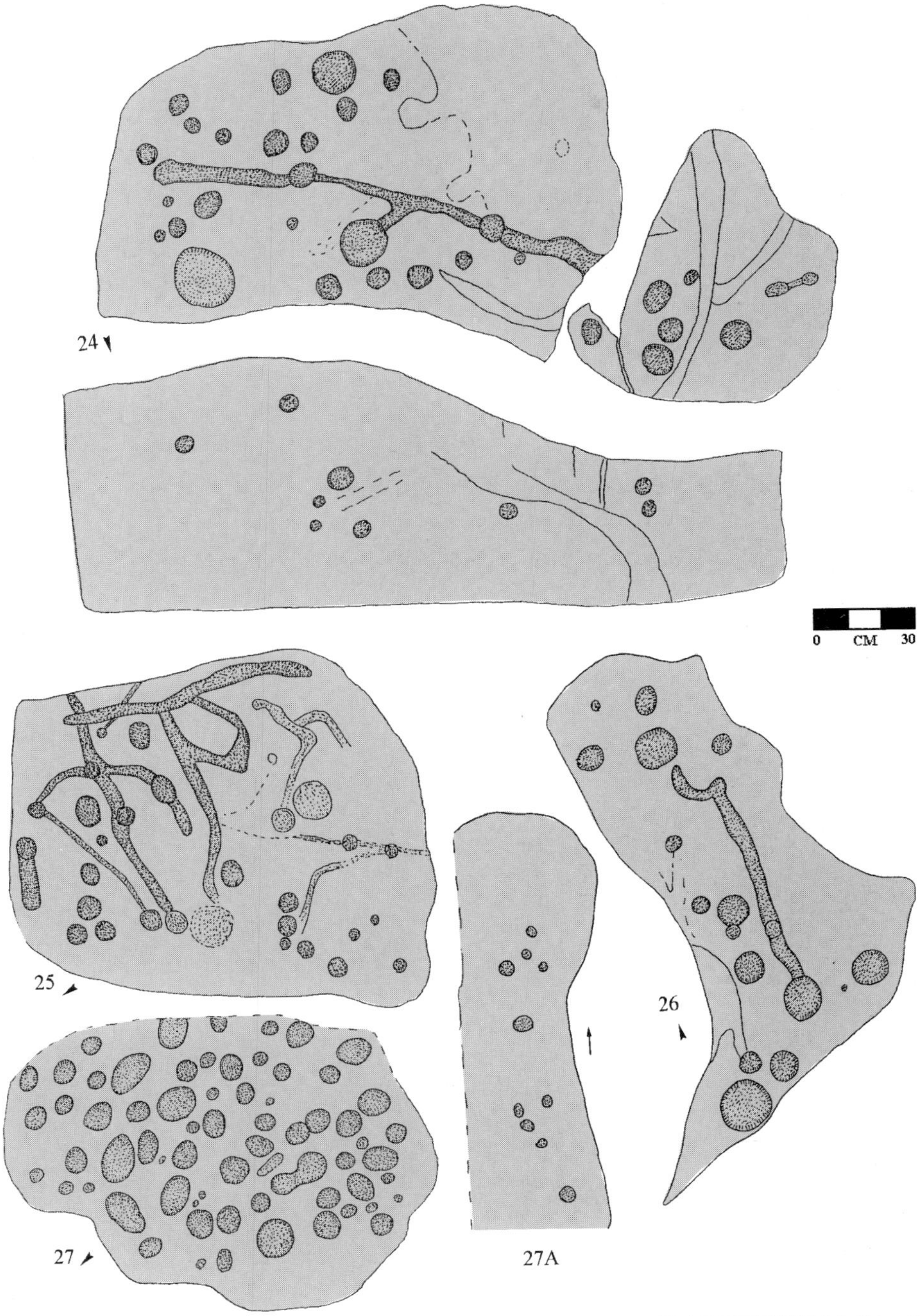


BARNINGHAM 24 - 27A

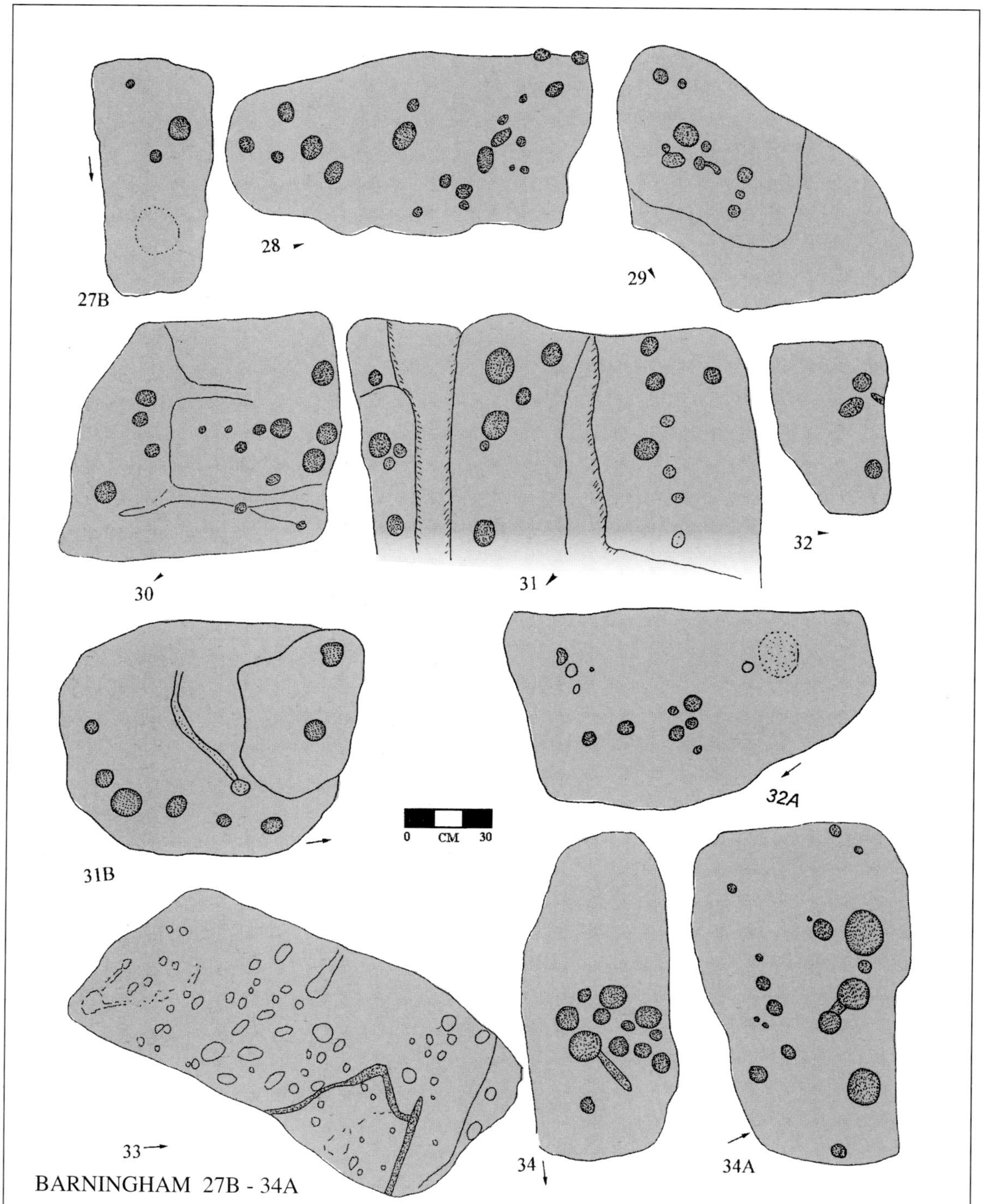

BARNINGHAM 27B - 34A

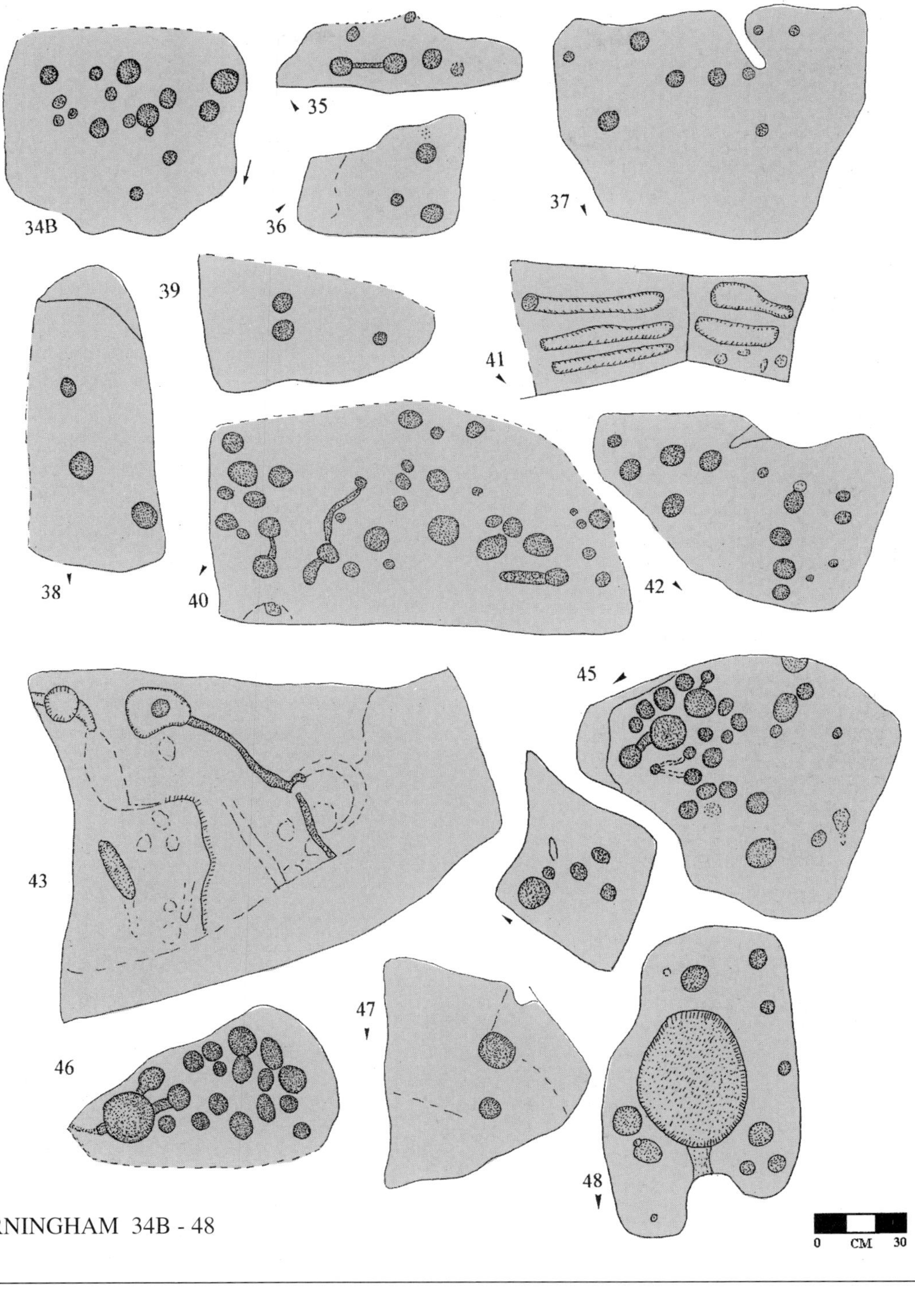


BARNINGHAM 34B - 48

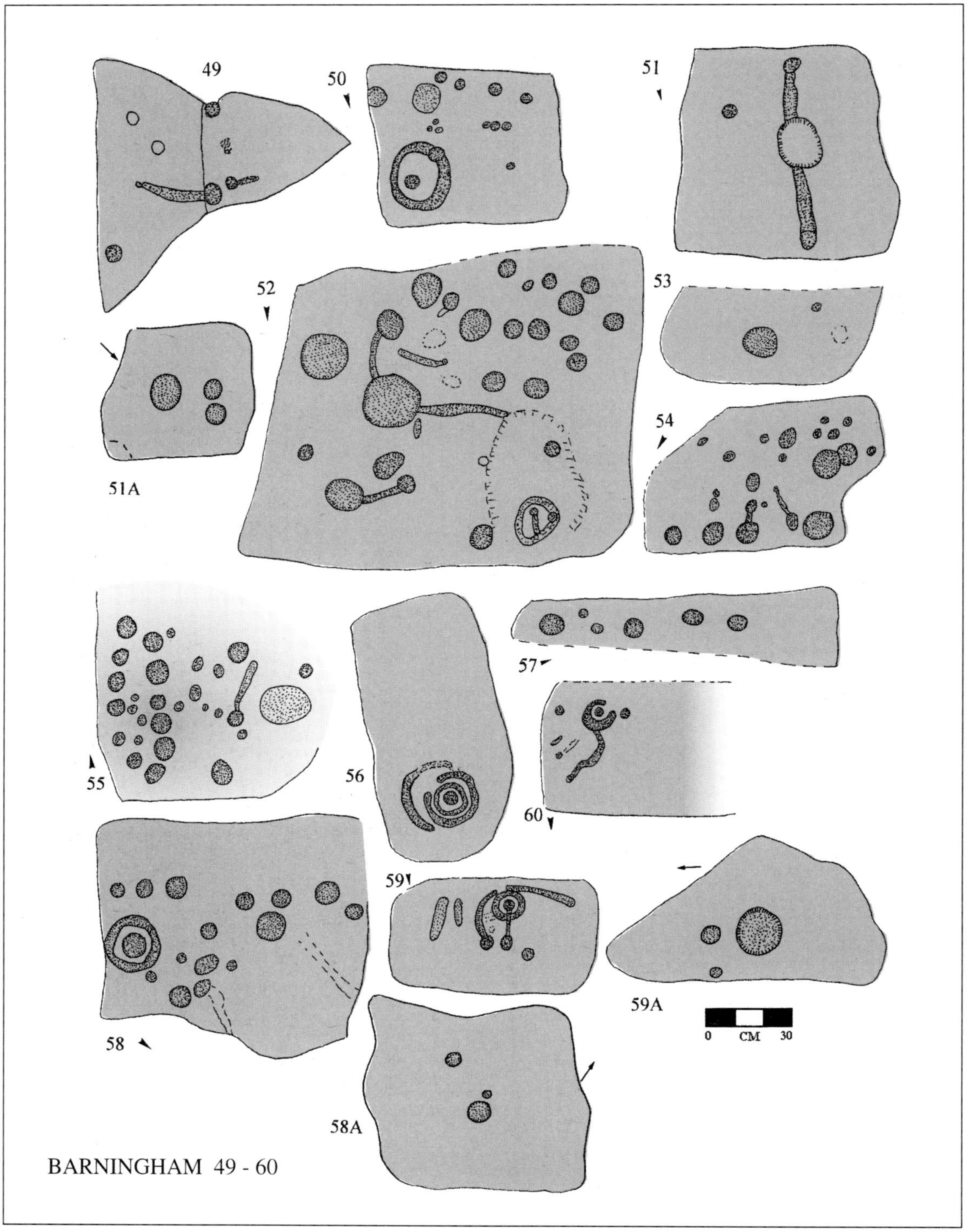


BARNINGHAM 49 - 60

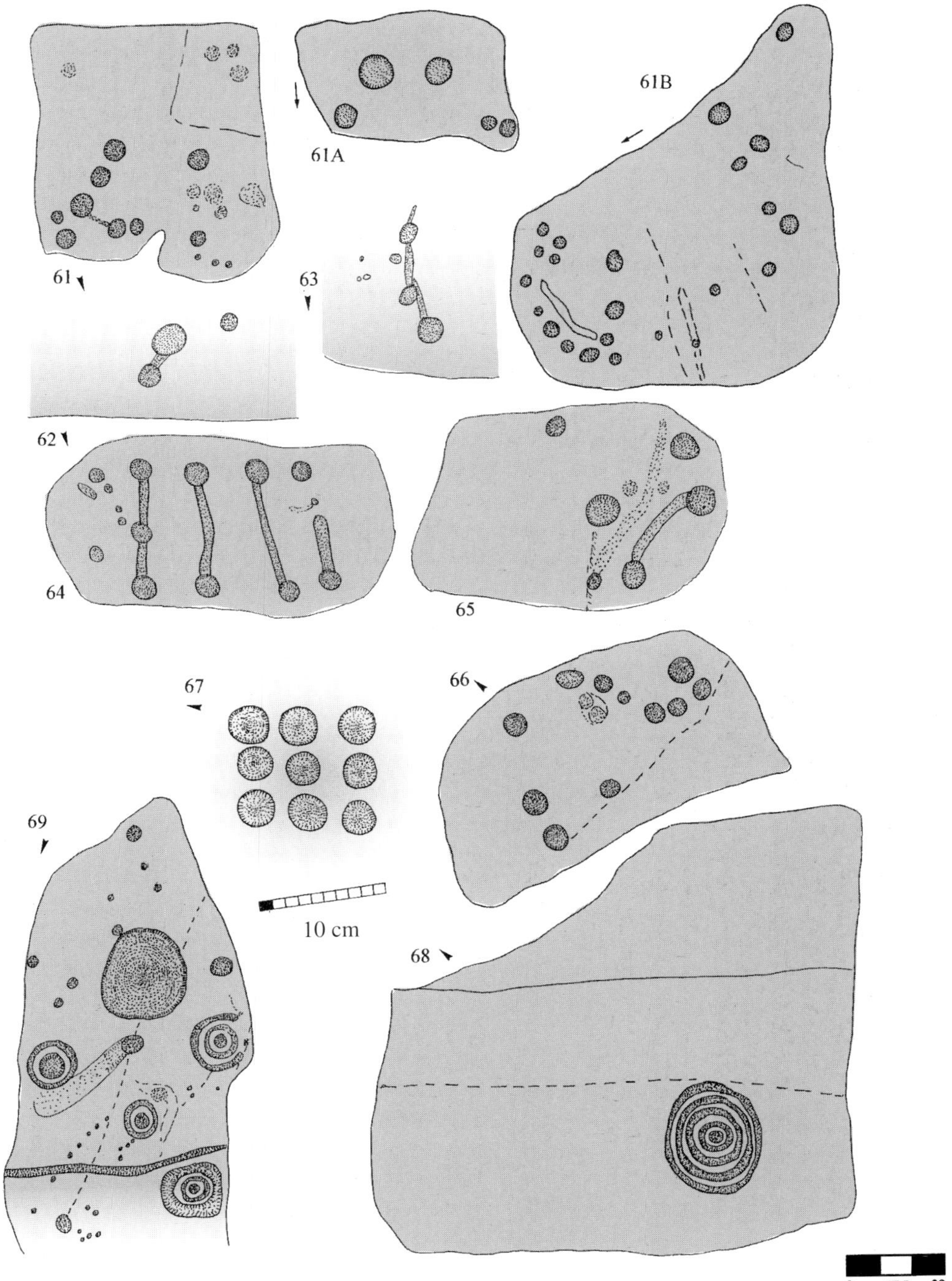

BARNINGHAM 61 - 69

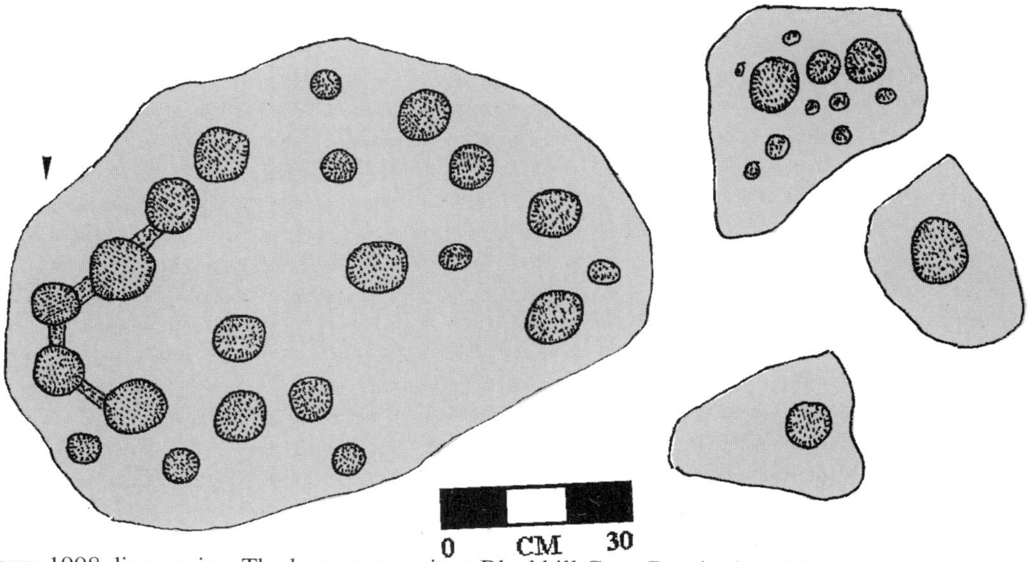


Above: 1998 discoveries: The largest stone is at Blackhill Gate, Barningham Moor (NZ 0446 0829). Top right are two cobbles, found in walls, now in Jack Blackburn's garden, and the small cobble is close to Aske Hall (NZ 1790 0405).

(Below) THE FRANKINSHAW CAIRN: with 3 marked rocks (78-80)

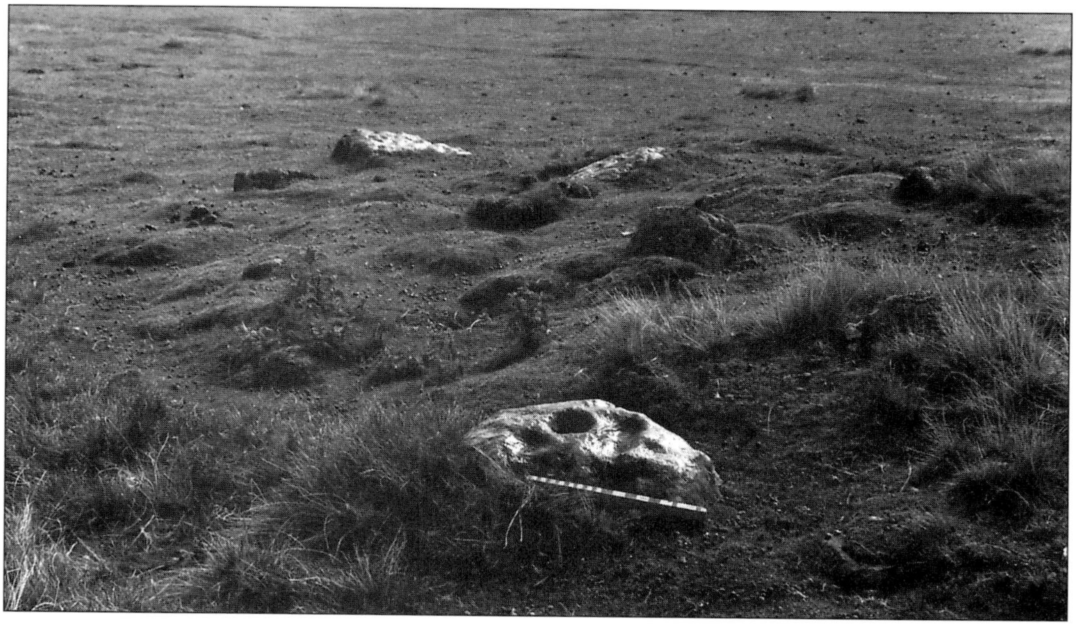

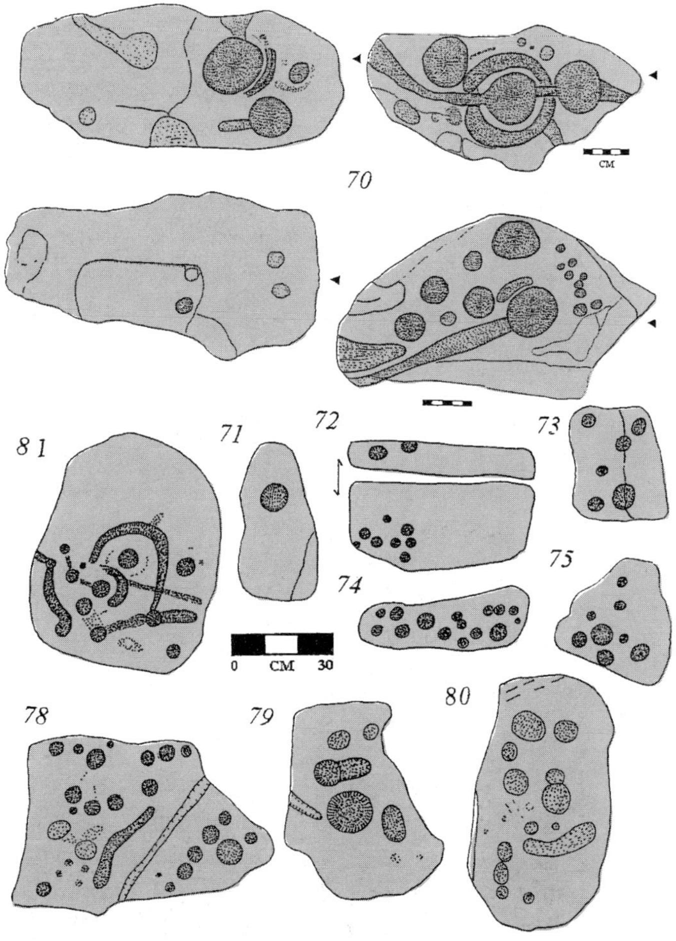


BARNINGHAM 70 - 81

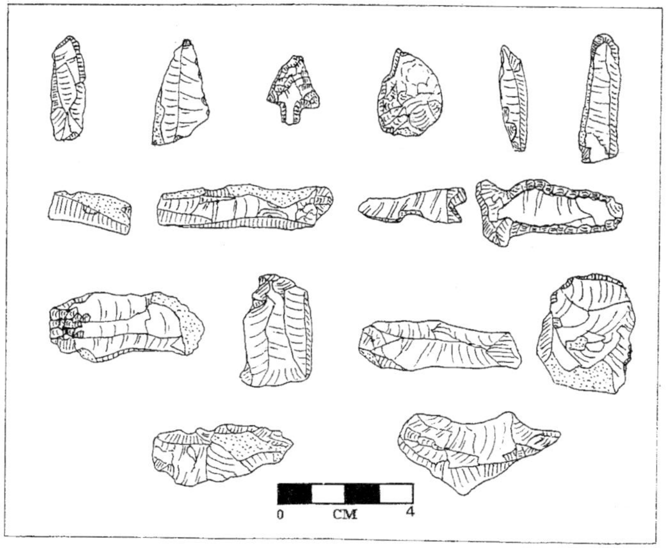


FLINTS WITH A WIDE TIME SPAN
AT FRANKINSHAW WELL.
*(Paul Brown)*

## (iii) Deepdale

Low Crag is aptly named: as you turn north off the Lartington Green Lane and walk the bridle road southwards to the site, you cross the Gill Beck by a small wood, and the fields on either side of the road rise to the south, reach a ridge, and gently slope away to the south, with their rig and furrow evidence of extensive clearance for arable. This open pasture ends with a wood and artificially-created Crag Pond that has a low outcrop of gritty sandstone to its north, running east to west approximately on the line of the public footpath. The bedrock at the entrance to this wood as the road goes on to Low Crag farm is only occasionally visible to the west in the thin grassland. Further east, away from the public path, the crag continues as a more massive outcrop that has the traces of rock carving, perhaps a fraction of what there used to be, and more may still be hidden.

As the rising fields to the north of Low Crag obscure the view in that direction, the sites look south, where there is an area of water, wood and marsh in a hollow, and this gives a strong clue as to why the motifs are there, for this long stretch of swamp may have been a watering hole and the home of marsh birds. Thus the crag overlooks an important source of food before the land rises slightly again with more rock outcrops, then drops dramatically into the Deepdale valley.

The first marked rock is situated just west of the track before it enters the wood, close to the wall that encloses the wood, and visible from the trackway, on the line of the footpath. Here there is a flat outcrop (1) that is covered with cups, two long grooves, and two figures made up of linked cups, along its southern edge. To the east of the gate that lies beside the same trackway, on which the footpath arrow is mounted, are two rocks on either side of the gateway, numbers 2 (also found by Paul Brown) and 3. The rest of the motifs are on the continuation of the crag eastward, on private land. There are cups, some eroded, but there is also a rock with artificial grooves and cups on its sloping surface (4). A cup and single ring lies on the same outcrop a few metres further east (5). Rock 6 has deep connected cups, 7 continues on the same line as 4 and 5, and is marked with large cups from which grooves lead down the southern slope. Furthest east along the same outcrop is 8, a flat rock with natural cracks that have been enhanced to form wide grooves, with the addition of cups.

Across the marsh is a small cup mark on outcrop to the east (9), and by a modern wall next to Medieval rig and furrow and a long house is 10, a deep symmetrical basin and a faint cup on a protruding slab. It would be surprising if quarrying had not removed more marked rock, and at Denis Coggins' house, Low Crag, there are three small rocks, two with single cups and one with three, that have most likely been removed by quarrying and used in a wall. One feels that this is an area where more may be awaiting discovery, most likely by Mr. Coggins, who found most of the others. The designs are in all cases simple, with cups predominating, but their position on the edge of a possible swamp in Prehistoric times, with its animal and bird life, makes the location of great interest.

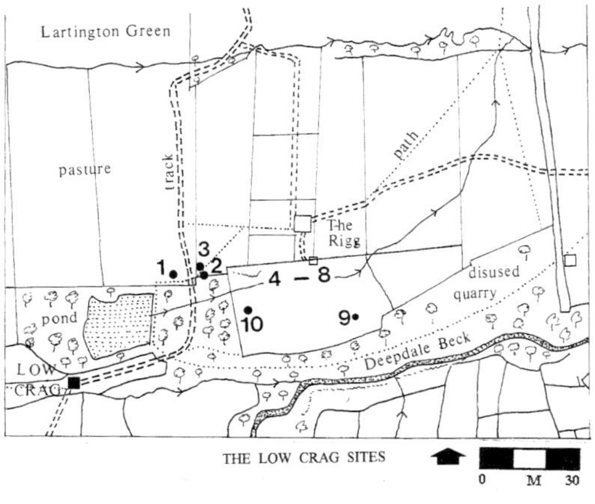

THE LOW CRAG SITES

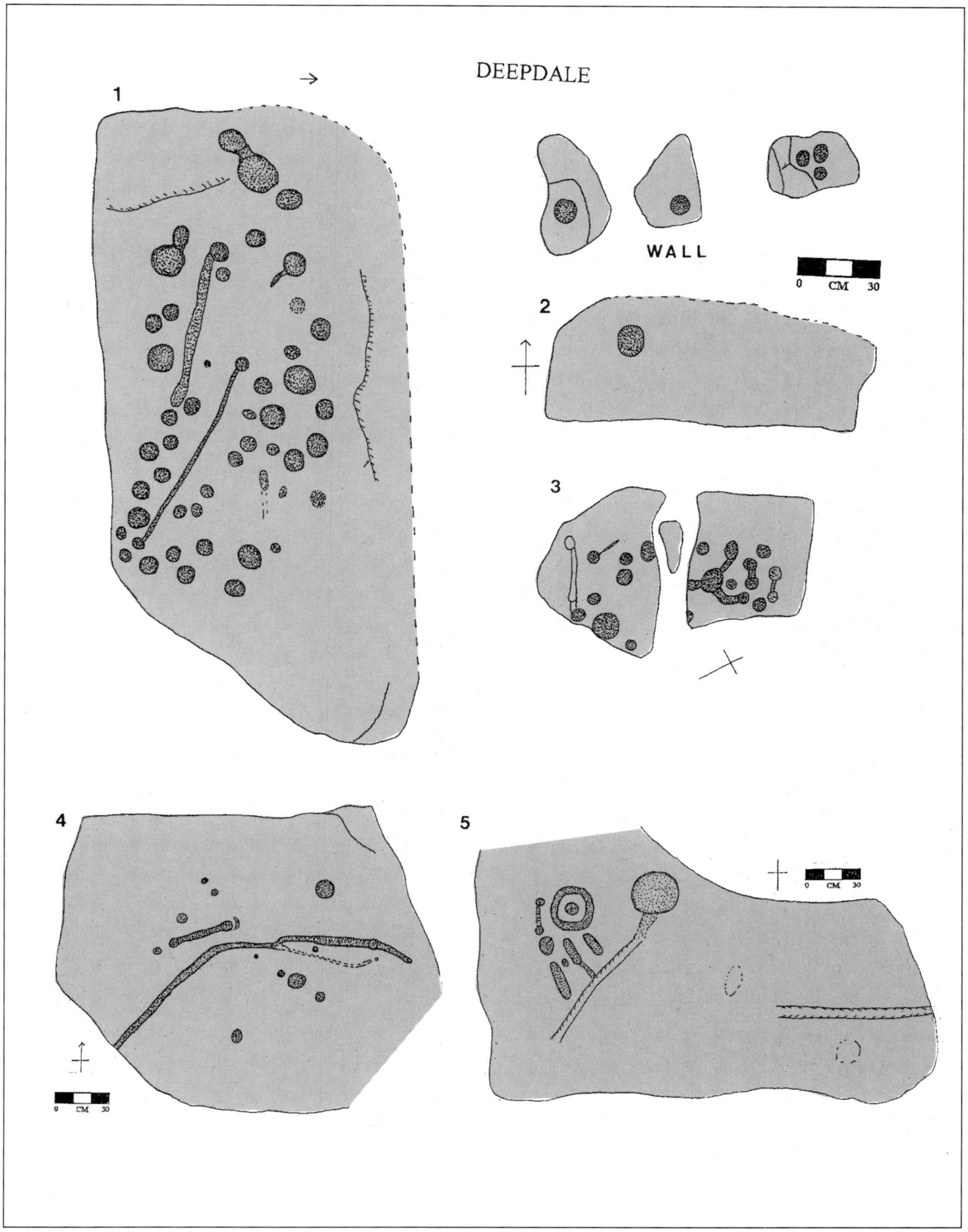
DEEPDALE
1
WALL
0 CM 30
2
3
4
0 CM 30
5
0 CM 30

DEEPDALE

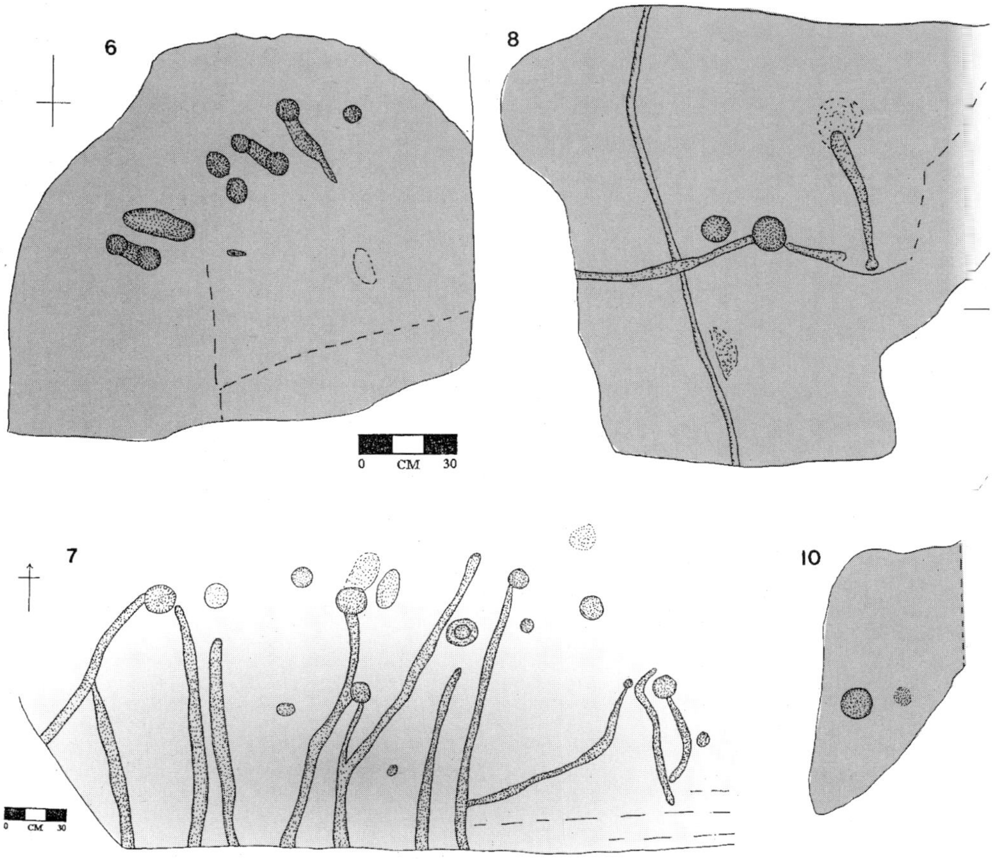


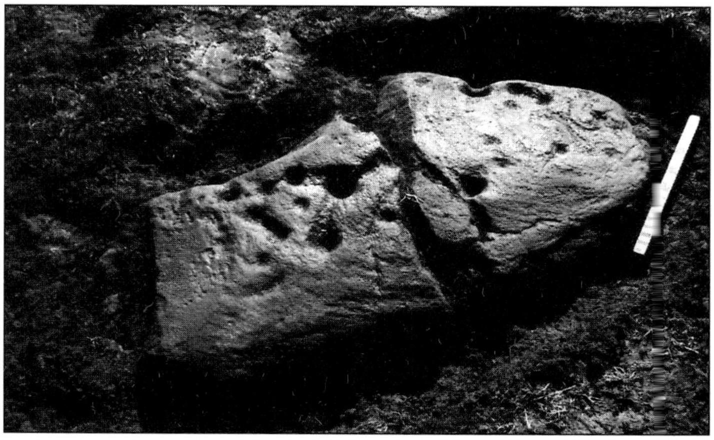

No. 3

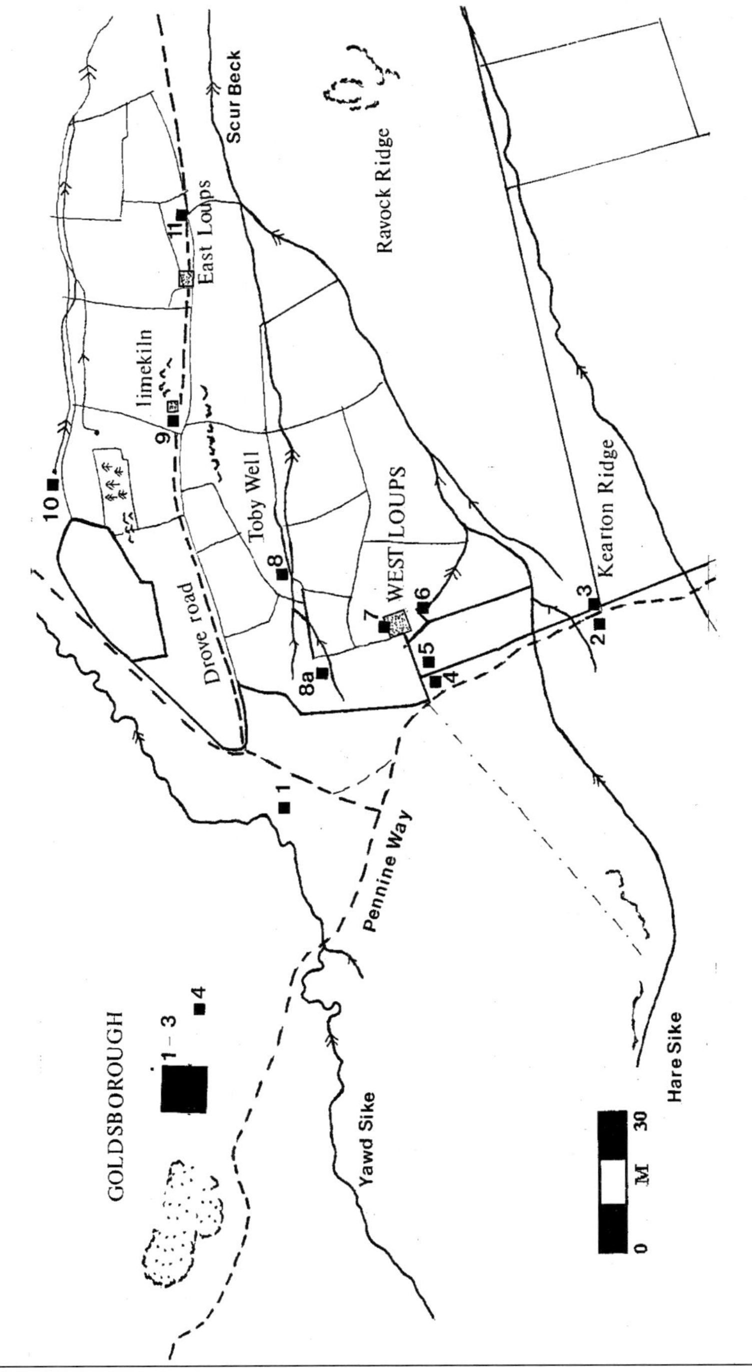


MAP OF THE GOLDSBOROUGH AND LOUPS SITES.

## (iv) Cotherstone Moor

The Cotherstone Moor group includes sites on the eastern ridge of Goldsborough, West and East Loups and three rocks on the Pennine Way. The sites were discovered by Denis Coggins and Louise Gidney. Stylistically, the motifs on these dispersed sites have much in common, but their positions in the landscape have different foci.

**Goldsborough**

The sandstone crags of Goldsborough do not have any sites, but the eastern ridge has earthfast slabs of gritty sandstone, some of which have motifs, and all of which give extensive viewpoints north and east to the main Tees lowlands.

**Rock 1:** The largest rock is furthest north of a group of three (1-3). The faults in the block have been used to form zones in which cups with single rings have been pecked into the gritty surface, and SW-NE downward slopes have been followed by artificial grooves.

The motifs are clearly pecked, and the gritstone has preserved them well.

**Rock 2:** about 6m west of 1 (240$^{0}$ ), still on the north edge of the spur, is a near -horizontal surface of gritstone that has what appears to be tentative/ unfinished motifs, the predominant idea being a central deep cup surrounded by a single ring. One figure has the beginnings of multiple rings, possibly three, but incomplete.

**Rock 3:** about 30m west up the hill from 2, this flat block has a pecked single ring around a cup from which a groove runs. Its outline has been lightly picked, but not worked on any more.

**Rock 4**: This isolated rock is furthest down the slope from 1-3, towards West Loups, and has parallel grooves that are pecked into a near-vertical face and two cups that are ringed by using natural features of the rock. Rock 4B lichen-covered, lies to the north of 4.

**West and East Loups.**

The West Loups rocks focus on a wide, shallow valley, with the motifs looking inwards and downwards into the valley, with special areas such as springs being pinpointed. Whereas there is nothing as yet to suggest settlement on the Goldsborough spur, the West Loups farmhouse site has had occupation that extends from an early circular enclosure containing an early medieval longhouse and partly enclosing the still-visible remains of a farmhouse dating from the 16th Century. In one sense the farm seems shut in by the valley, with a northern outcrop of sandstone forming a distinct ridge, but the view east is of a wide, gently-sloping valley broken at the east end by the Ravock Ridge. The motifs mark the margins of this area, with three in a special context, two at springs and one in an old enclosure.

**Rock 1**: This sandstone boulder, easily overlooked, lies on the steep slope to the stream. It has 35 cups of different sizes and depths. The position of the rock may not be its original one, unless it was a marker on a path that led across the stream valley .

**Rock 2**: This sloping block lies on the west side of the Pennine Way, below the southern ridge (thus limiting the viewpoint on the south side), on Kearton Rigg. It inclines to the vertical, and has a uniform surface with fine horizontal cracks. It supports a line of four cups with single rings. A striking feature is that grooves are pecked to run down the steep slope, crossed by a horizontal groove, enclosing an area that has been covered with tiny pick marks, a surface preparation which is unique in this area. The surface with cups, rings and grooves does not appear to have been eroded. There are other cup marks, including one on the thickness of the rock to the north, and a deep cut which may be natural.

**Rock 3**: This lies opposite Rock 2, by the Pennine Way. Its cups and grooves are obscured by vegetation.

**Rock 4**: This horizontal, uniform block of sandstone is marked with large cups, a cup and a pennannular, and a cluster of four cups with a near-circular groove, a design unique to this area.

To the east of the Pennine way, access is strictly limited in a Military Danger area, usually open to the public, with permission, on a Sunday afternoon. It was once a sheltered farmstead, and there was much quarrying for sandstone and lime. Rig and furrow is still evident, old boundary walls, and an impressive linear banked Drove road.

**Rock 5**: This is a horizontal outcrop, with a cup and ring that makes use of a small natural dome in the rock, another ringed cup, and two cups with arcs.

**Rock 6**: This is a boulder almost buried in a narrow stream bed near the spring source.

**Rock 7**: This stone lies inside the circular enclosure that pre-dates the farm, close to the farm wall. To the north is massive outcrop, some of its horizontal surface having large countersunk cups (8a), and to the east of this is 8, at Toby Well, a spring. Further north across the drove road, and close to a lime kiln is 9, on a large slab sloping into the next valley, and on the opposite side of the same valley is 10.The farm track eastward from here, with its impressive linear banks, passes a ruined late 19th century farmhouse and at the farm gate a block of sandstone has a wall built on its horizontal surface, covering cup marks (11). On the same surface the initials JW and 1959 may well have been added by a soldier. This outcrop is particularly striking, as it is a dominant viewpoint, looking south and east into the Scur Beck valley. It is impossible to say how old the droveway is, but its course on a ridge may be older than its present embanked form.

This strange, remote area is unfortunately inaccessible most of the time, but its use by the military has in some ways preserved it. It has great evocative character which will appeal to many sides of our nature.

## (v) Blake Hill to Eggleston

**Marwood (NZ 0391 1915)**
Denis Coggins and Dr. Ken Fairless found an isolated cup marked earthfast sandstone just visible above the grass. It lies on Knott Hill, NW of the site of the deserted village of Marwood, looking SE to the River Tees valley.

**Overlooking Baldersdale to the South**
The Blake Hill-Scaletree Plantation sites lie north of a minor road from Romaldkirk via Hunderthwaite to the Blackton and Balderhead Reservoirs. They stand on a ridge of sandstone aligned roughly east-west overlooking Baldersdale to the south, at approximately 360m. The most westerly site is Blake Hill, south of the planted forest (Brownberry) at the corner of which (marked by a concrete pillar) are abandoned quarry workings. It is a round hill at 367m with all-round visibility from the top, on which there are animal feed troughs. Some boulders lie on the edge of the knoll, ice borne, but only the four on the south side are marked.

Further east is a single cup rock on the edge of an enclosure of indeterminate date. The only rock recorded on the OS is 7, a slab with many cups on an elongated hill NE of Briar Dykes farm. Two more can be added: 8, a small cupped slab, found by Paul Brown, and 6 which lies below the ridge just north of a linear earthwork, found during the recent EH survey. In the next field east are the How Gill rocks, only recorded in 1998, and found

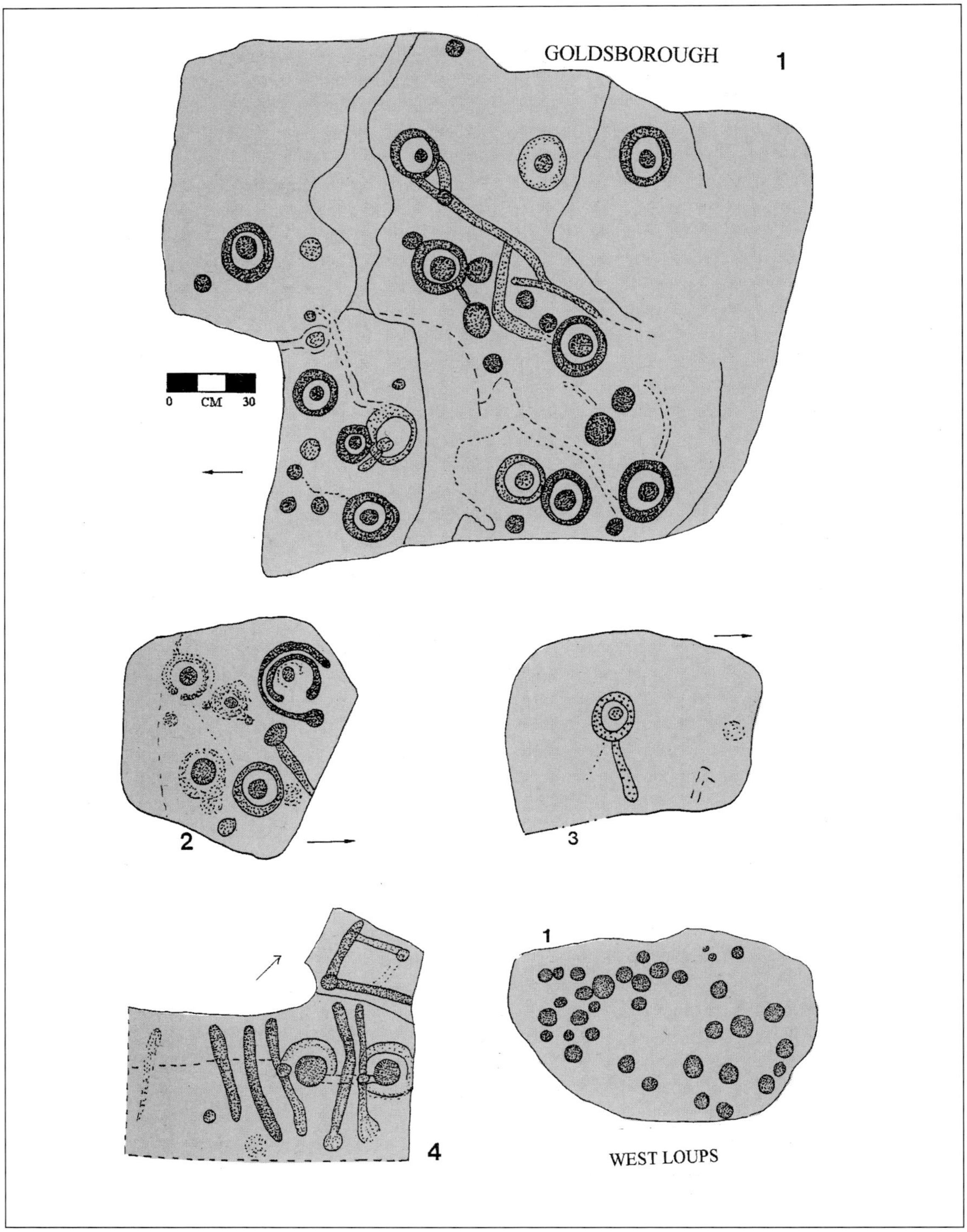
GOLDSBOROUGH
1
0 CM 30
2
3
4
1
WEST LOUPS

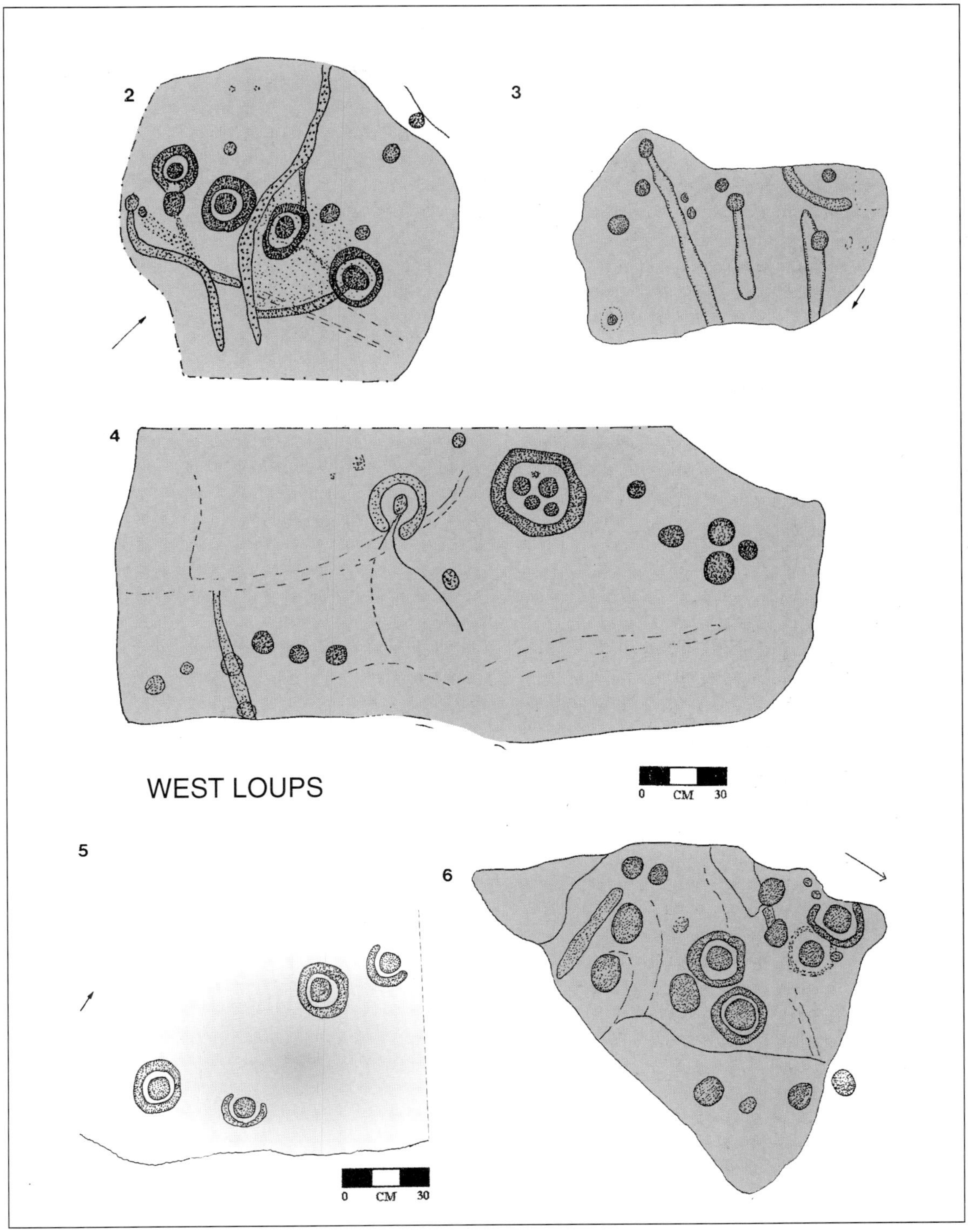
2
3
4
WEST LOUPS
0 CM 30
5
6
0 CM 30

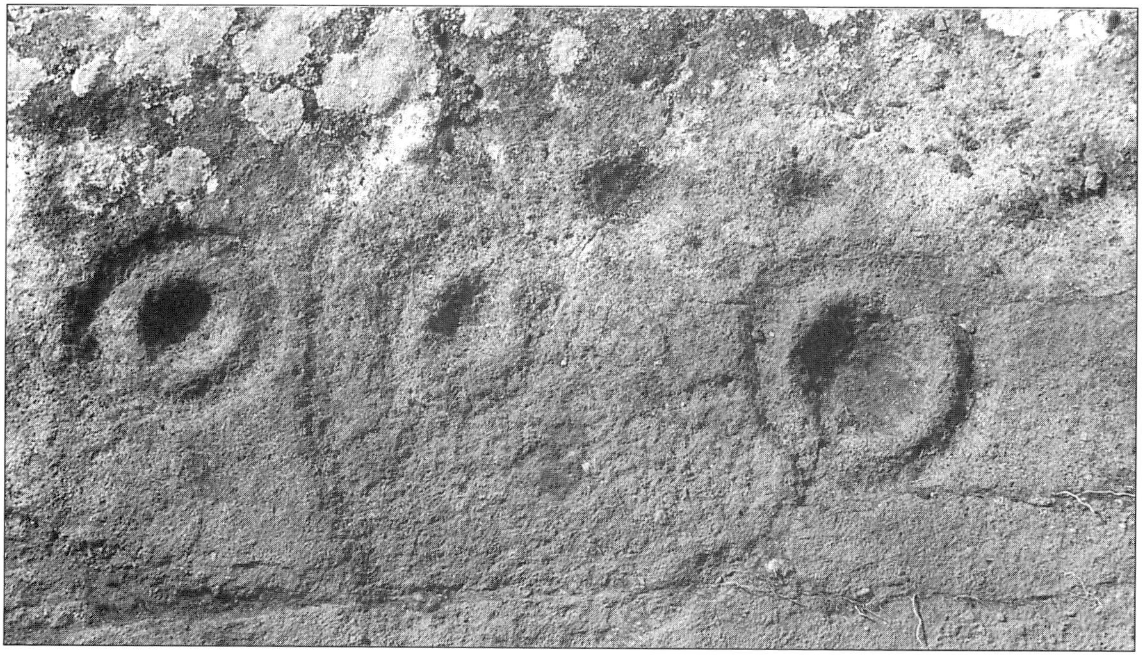

WEST LOUPS: The position and markings of rock 2. It lies on the Pennine Way seen to the right, and is marked with a black triangle.

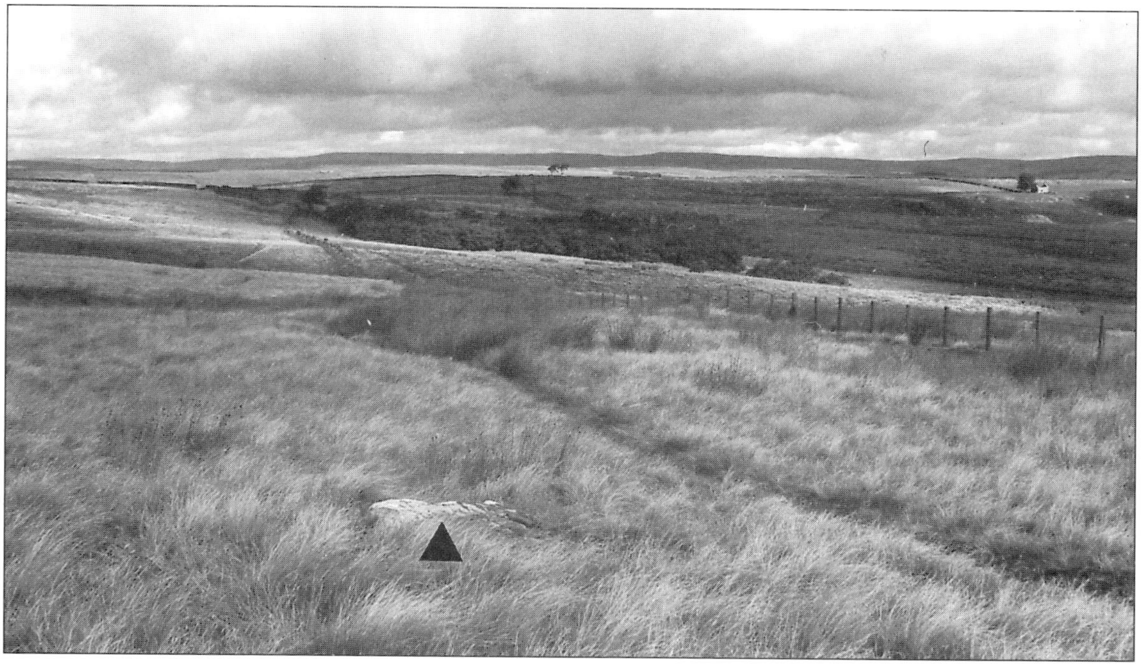

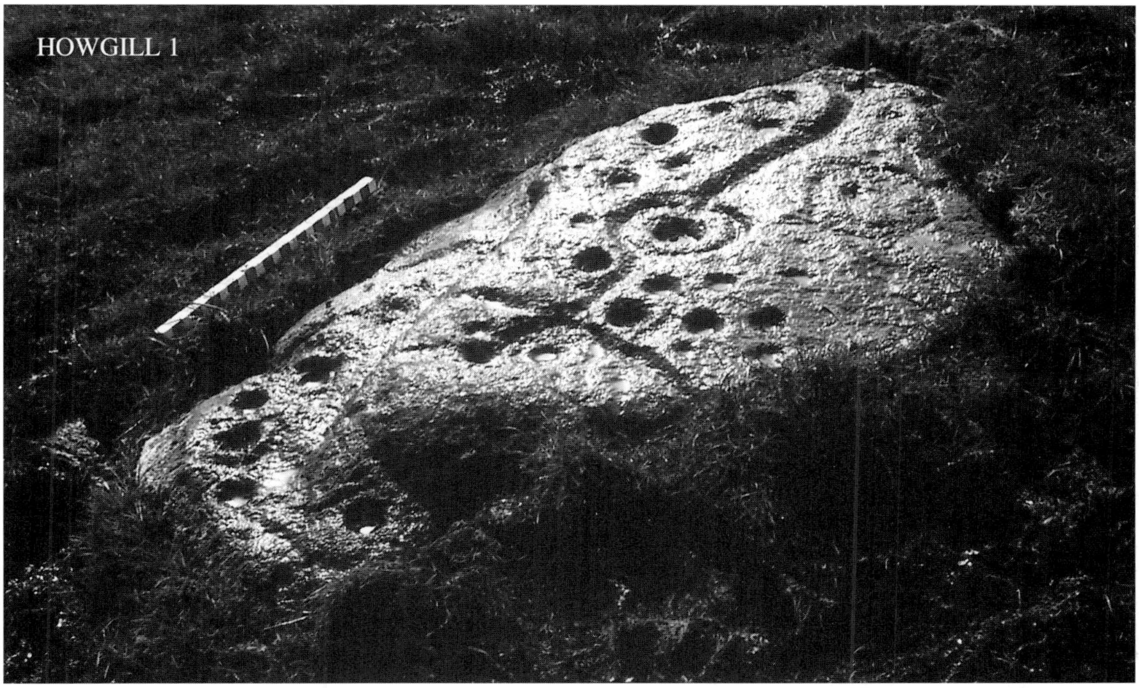

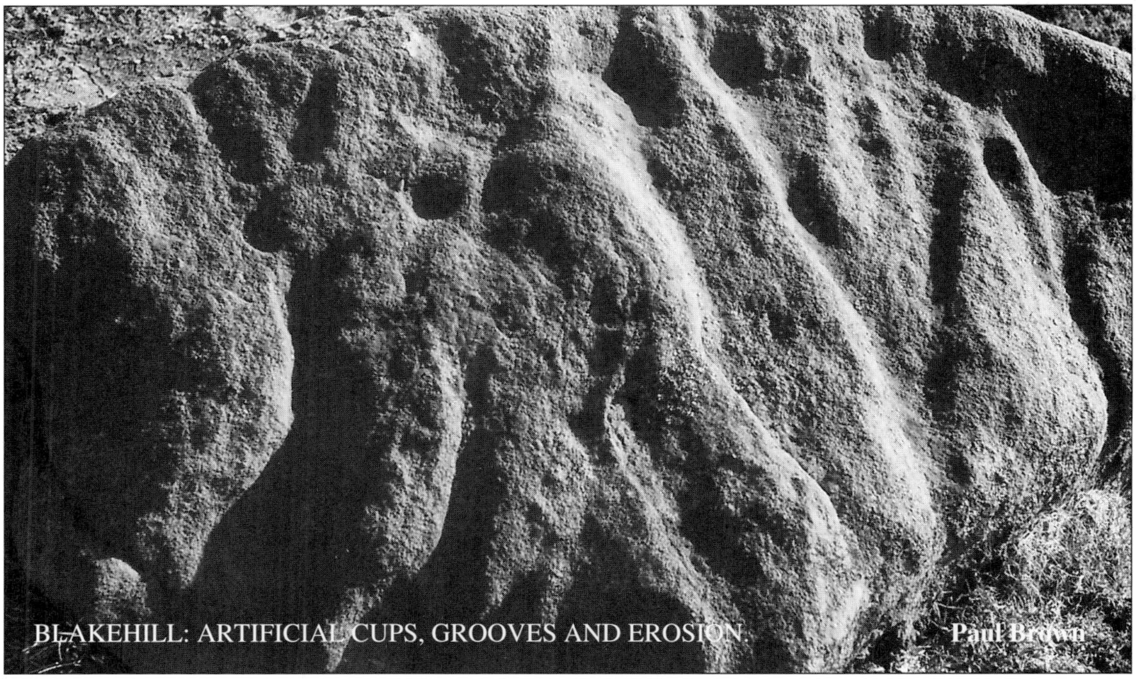

by P. Brown and B. Mclean. 1 is particularly striking, a complex design picked out of rough Millstone grit. Its position is odd, for it lies on a flat, very marshy pasture, along with 2, which has only a few cups, one with a penannular ring. It could be that they mark the beginnings of springs. 3 is close by, a large grit slab with deeply picked cups.

On the ridge to the North, beyond the continuation of the linear earthwork, is a ridge with 4 at the best viewpoint, but with the more elaborate 5 on the even top surface. There are several cairns on this ridge, which has an extensive view across the Baldersdale valley to the Goldsborough and Loups sites, where the type of rock and motifs are so similar. All the sites are on private land, and the farmers have been most supportive of our recording. Further east on the edge of Scaletree Plantation are two marked rocks, found by J. Pickin, one with rings. They are on a public footpath, and one is illustrated.

**Eggleston and Langleydale Common**

The work of an individual can often change significantly the picture of the distribution of rock art, and sometimes the density of finds is in proportion to the enthusiasm and hard work of local fieldworkers. Paul Brown, acting on an obscure reference to a decorated rock in the area of Eggleston village, has now revealed many new sites on high moorland north of the Tees, where none was known previously. He has been helped in his search by Barbara Mclean and Michael Gibbs. The long hours spent by Paul searching through museum records, newspaper archives, and field walking the area reads like a detective story! The full story of his discoveries will be the subject of a forthcoming paper.

All but one of the sites are bounded to the south and south east by the B6282 from Eggleston to the Woolly Hills, including part of Barnard Castle Allotment and Langleydale Common, with a southern outlier near Hindon Edge. This is a long ridge of gritty sandstone, with impressive bell pits, quarries, coarse grass, sheep, grouse and not much else today. It is cut up into steep valleys with small streams flowing north and south from the watershed. The highest marked rock is at about 420m on Langleydale Common, and the lowest at about 340m.

All of the land is private, mostly owned by Raby Estate, patrolled always by gamekeepers, so this information has only been made accessible by a careful approach to landowners. The rock art is very simple, based almost entirely on cups. Although some rocks have extensive views over the landscape, others are placed in what appears to be a more specialised use of the land. Other rocks illustrated reveal the same simple use of small rock surfaces: cups and some grooves being the order of the day. As there is nothing yet with which to associate them in time or culture, suffice it to say that their very presence has only just been revealed and that the types of motifs are quite simple. This is the first time that this new scatter of marked rocks has been published.

**Eastern sites**

The thin scatter of marked rocks spreads over Langleydale Common, but the use of the land for grouse restricts access. However, the boulders and earthfast slabs that are marked have very simple scatters of cups mainly, all placed so that they overlook valleys. From the east Langleydale Common sites the single marked rock on the top of Woolly Hill is visible: an impressive situation of wide views from the edge of a natural oval-shaped platform at the top of a hill. The largest rock is an isolated outcrop at Hindon Edge that is visible from the north and overlooks the Tees valley and Barnard Castle to the south. The rock and its position are impressive, and overlook faint traces of cairns and field walls. At first sight

Eggleston and Langleydale Common

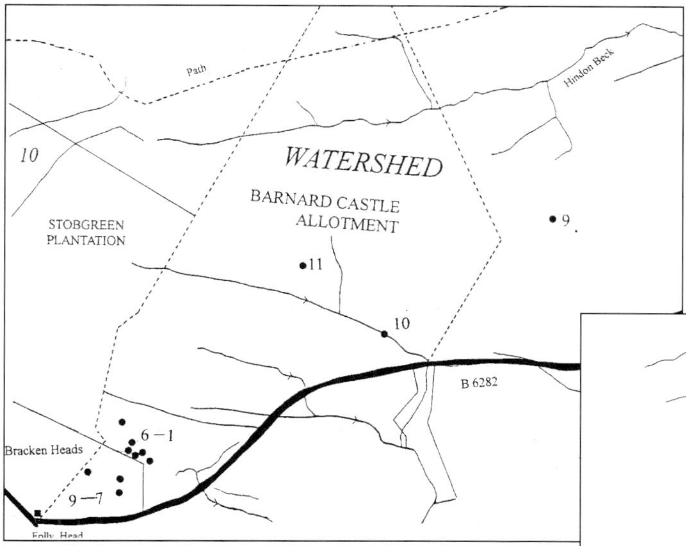


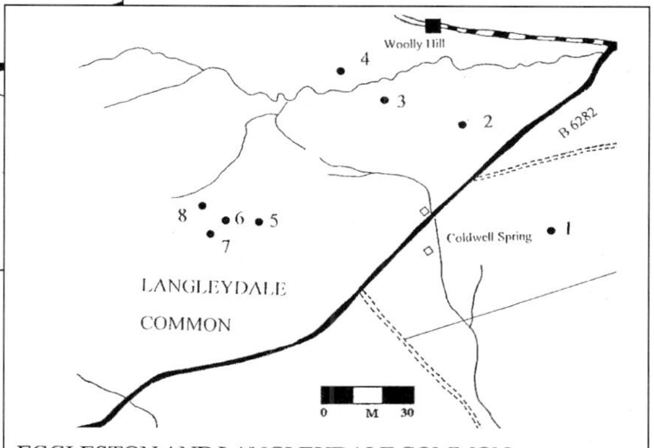

EGGLESTON AND LANGLEYDALE COMMON

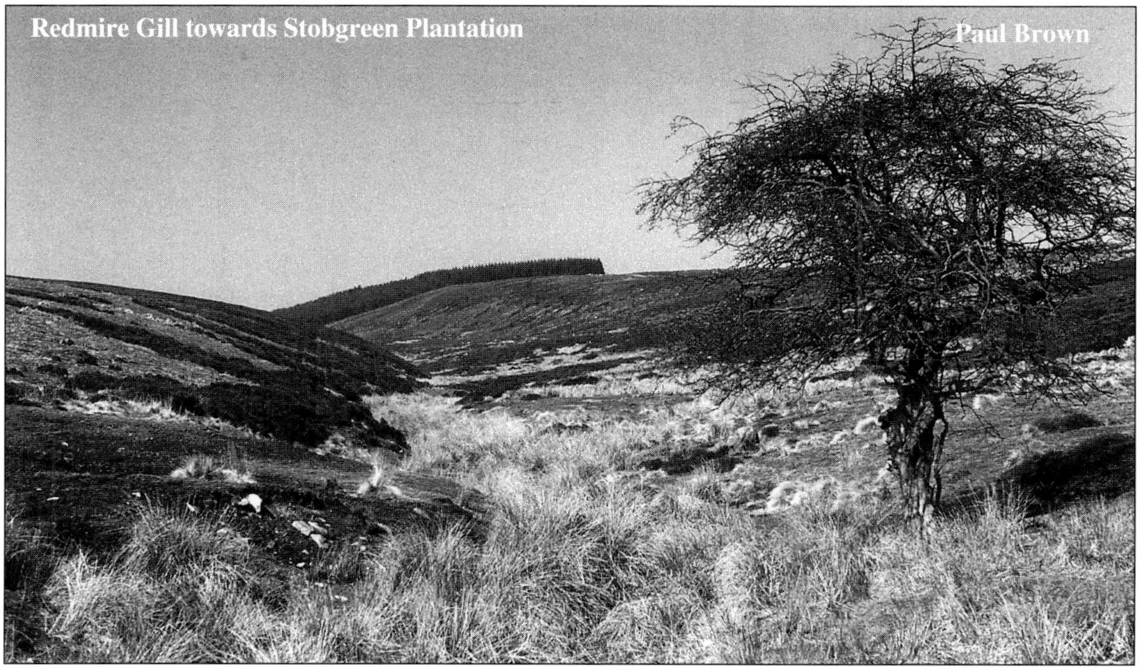
Redmire Gill towards Stobgreen Plantation
Paul Brown

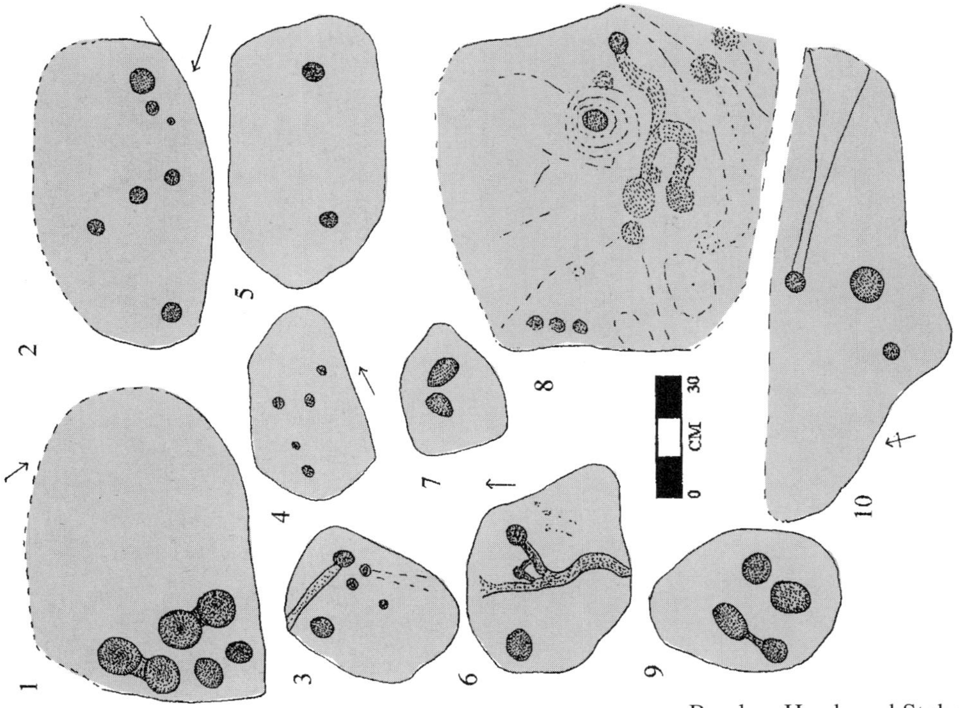


Bracken Heads and Stobgreen

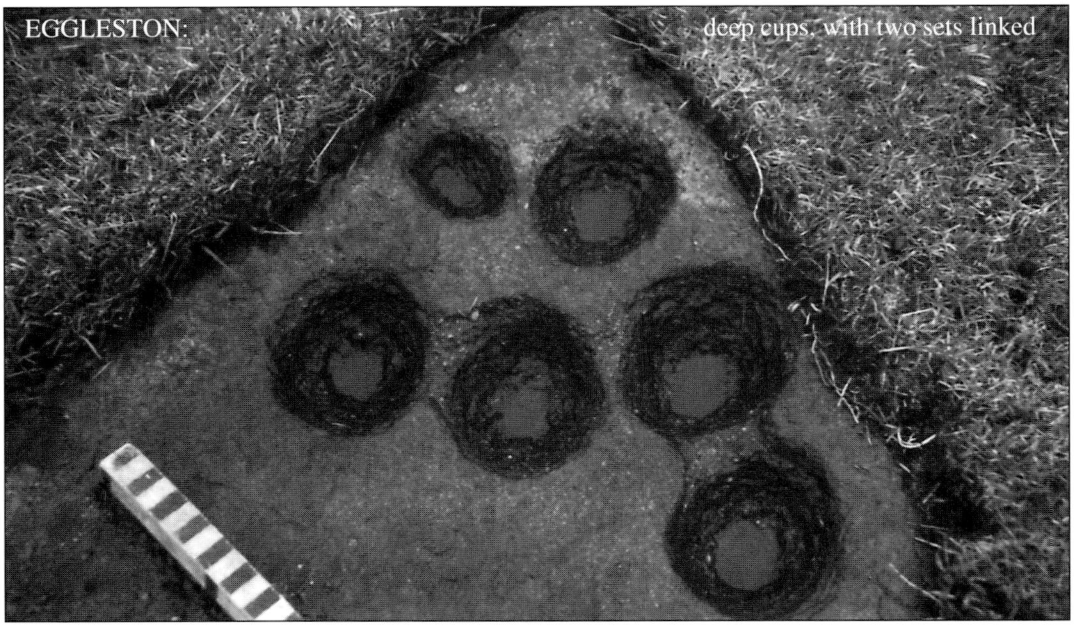

EGGLESTON: deep cups, with two sets linked

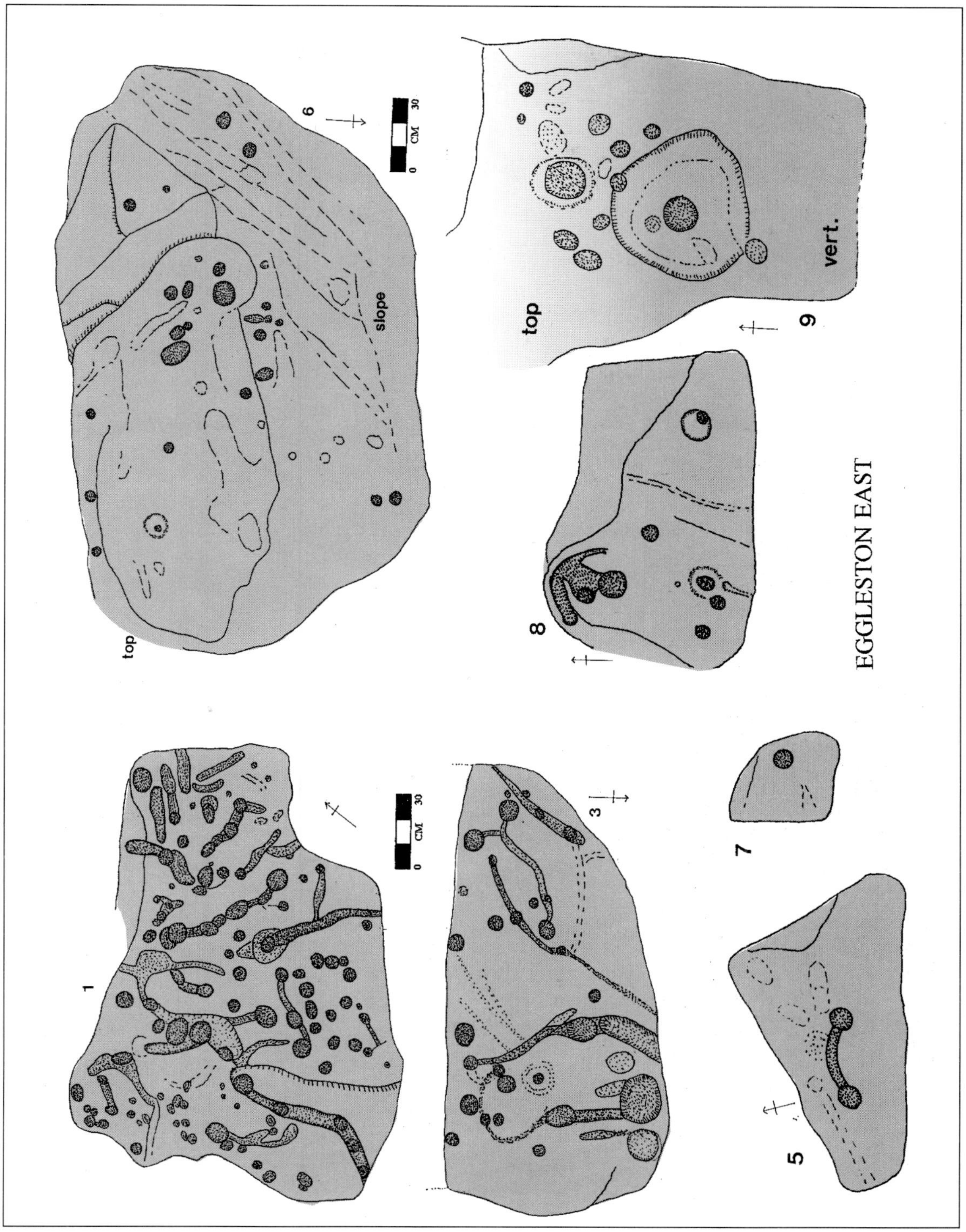
EGGLESTON EAST
1
3
5
6
7
8
9
top
slope
top
vert.
0 CM 30
0 CM 30

there does not appear to be much on this small table-like rock, but careful work has revealed a large number of cups, many strung together to form grooves. The significance of the area may be greater than first thought. South of the carved rock Paul Brown and Michael Gibbs made the discovery of a stone-lined cist. This was excavated by Niall Hammond of Durham County Council in 1997 and revealed a well-preserved beaker burial, one of only 5 examples known from the county. In the same area as the cist, survey further identified a number of cairns in various states of preservation.

**Bracken Heads**

Seen from the road, the land changes from low-lying swampy ground to high ground that has been ploughed with wide rigg and furrow where it slopes to Folly Head. It is on this slope that a small four-cupped stone (9) occupies a prominent place, then there is a small valley, with a quarry in it, and the ridge above this valley is a spur with cairns and aligned stones. The next small valley has been scraped clear of stone, which may account for some of the cairns, and the floor is narrowly plough-ridged, a sign of small-scale arable use. The next ridge up has a small, walled enclosure with two round-house foundations and more cairns, and this overlooks the next cluster of rock markings. This main concentration is at a site south of Bracken Heads (6-1) and west of a disused quarry. A group of five marked boulders, now earthfast, marks the northern upper end of a small blind valley through which a stream runs, its source being a spring just below the marked rocks. The land in the depression is marshy. There are remnants of low old field walls leading up to the head of this valley. It creates, like Osmonds Gill on Barningham Moor and Low Crag at Lartington, a restricted area where beasts could be herded or trapped. Here and at Low Crag the marsh may have been a small lake in prehistoric times. Thus an important source of food may have prompted people to mark the site that overlooked the valuable area.

The cup marks are small, apart from 1, which has some of the largest, deepest, and best executed in the region. All are covered over with thin grass. There are cups and grooves (6) on an exposed stone to the NE, higher up the hill, with more extensive views, including rocks 1-5. There are also cairns, some dug out in the centre, and one has the remains of a cist inside it, filled with large boulders, and probably representing the curiosity of quarrymen in the area. A long cairn is also a possibility.

Rocks 10-12 are hidden in the Stobgreen Plantation, which also contains the stone that we call the Grayson stone, that led to the search for others. The story is interesting, and will be given in more detail in a forthcoming paper by Paul Brown. Mr. J.N. Grayson, a forestry worker, located a cup and ring stone in 1954 with a saddle quern nearby. Reports that the stone had been moved to a museum did not lead to its discovery, but Mr. Grayson and Mr. Wigston have given an account of how they discovered it during deep ploughing, when the plough hit an earthfast rock 2m long and 1m wide. More interesting information about such disturbance has emerged since, concerning the discovery of many worked flints, including arrow points and scrapers in the same area. The rock seems to have complex motifs in contrast to the simple cups that characterise the rest of the area.

## (vi) Isolated Stones:

**The Bowes Museum, private collections, and others**

There are 11 stones in the Bowes museum, in private collections, and in the field, all listed below:

**The Gainford stone**: this large slab is particularly important not only in the variety of its motifs, but because they occur on both sides. It was found during deep drainage excavations. An uneven top surface has been used partly by taking advantage of the irregularities. Long grooves divide the surface into 4 areas, each occupied by cups, some surrounded by from one to four concentric circles. There are signs of weathering. Some of the grooves are very finely pecked in the lower RHS, and very close together where the surface of the rock is smoothest. The top RHS shows more signs of erosion, as though that part of the rock had been exposed to weathering. The LHS, at a lower level has bolder and cruder technique, but the pick markings show that none of it was exposed to erosion. The intention of the motif-makers has been to use as much of the rock as possible: it is very 'busy'. There is also a strong sense of fluidity, of interconnection of cups to grooves and grooves to grooves.

The obverse side is quite different It is slightly domed, and the motifs, cups and grooves, are well spaced. The concept is much simpler, with clear pick marks. Some pick marks are very light, showing signs, at the lower RHS particularly, that they were toying with the idea of adding a ring or two. This is a likely candidate for a cist cover, but whether the more elaborate pattern was to face downwards or not is unclear. The idea of marking two sides in a different way is well illustrated by this and the Fulforth Farm stone.

**The Greta Bridge stone** was found during the widening of the A66, 400m east of the Roman fort, and had been re-used as a cover for a Roman burial. It has much in common with the simple designs in the area generally, the main motifs being well-defined cups and some connecting grooves, but there is at the top of the rock an arrangement of grooves that looks like an attempt to produce chevrons, but they are curved rather than angular. This type of motif is unusual in Britain, and seen in some Neolithic passage grave traditions.

**The Winston Station stone** is a cup marked small boulder found near to a mound. The cup is quite large for the size of the stone: 6.5cm wide and 2.5cm deep. It is now in the Bowes Museum (Ref.1994.5, at NZ 1445 1765).

**The Folly Plantation stone**, recorded under Gayles Moor, is in the Bowes Museum.

**The Dalton stone** which is in the Museum is a small, rounded boulder with a perfectly-made motif of central cup surrounded by a ring and two concentric penannulars, and the cup has a curved groove leading to another single cup.

Two further stones from **Dalton**, previously in Jack Blackburn's garden, are now on loan to the Bowes Museum. One triangular-shaped stone chosen for its shape is decorated on three sides. It is the object of careful design, and may have come from a special context, such as a burial. The flat sandstone slab has cups on either side, not elaborate in design, but it had a function outside the realm of earthfast marked rocks. It was found in a wall. Again, one suspects that it may have been in a monument. The find spots of these stones below the moorland and on more fertile soil may point to a use unlike that of the earthfasts on the high ground; a monumental function.

The three stones from Dalton were exhibited for all to see in Durham as part of the Visual Arts Year 1996 exhibition, two of them for the first time.

Top: The Gainford Cist Cover
Middle: Dalton
Bottom:
The Greta Bridge Stone

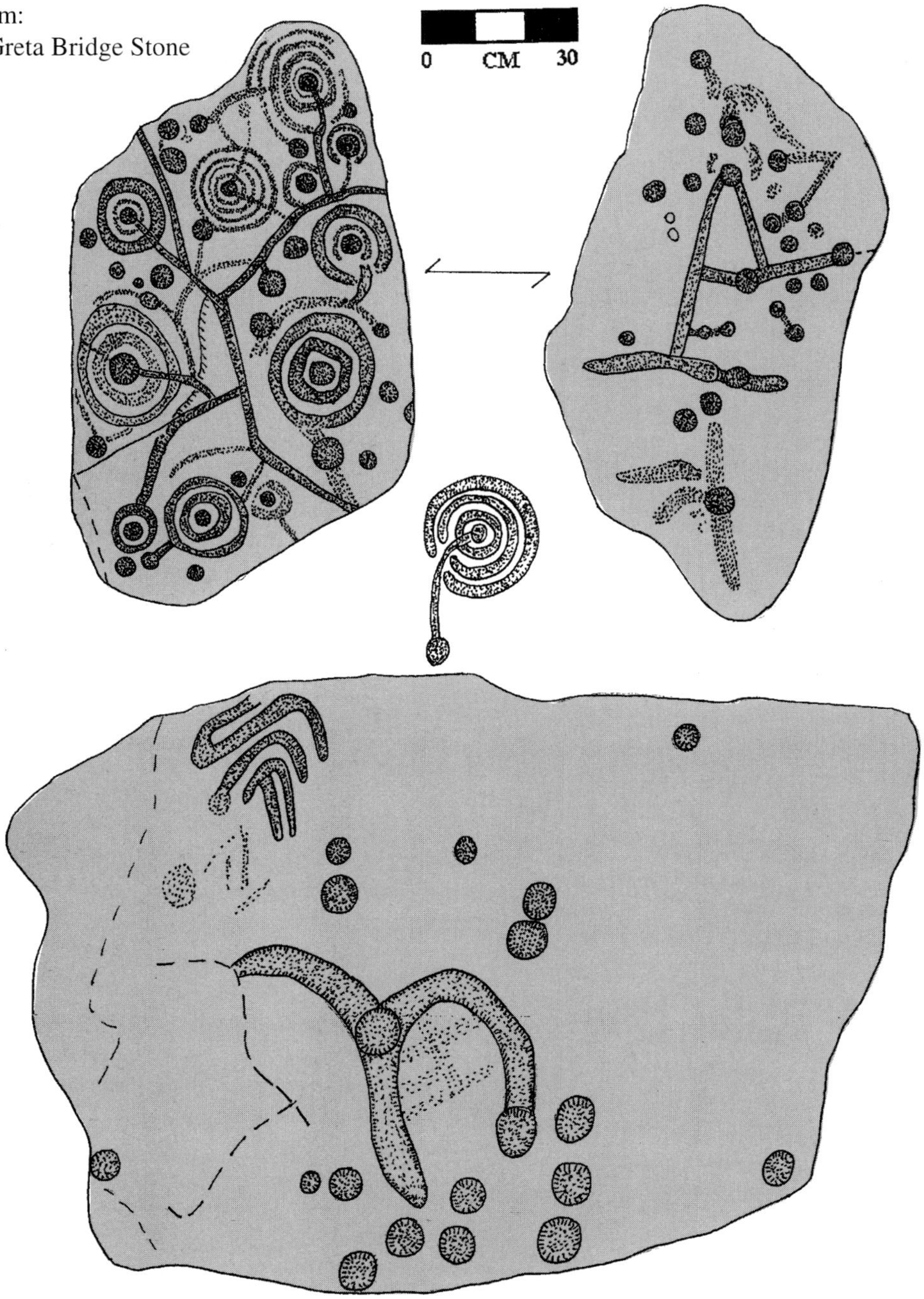

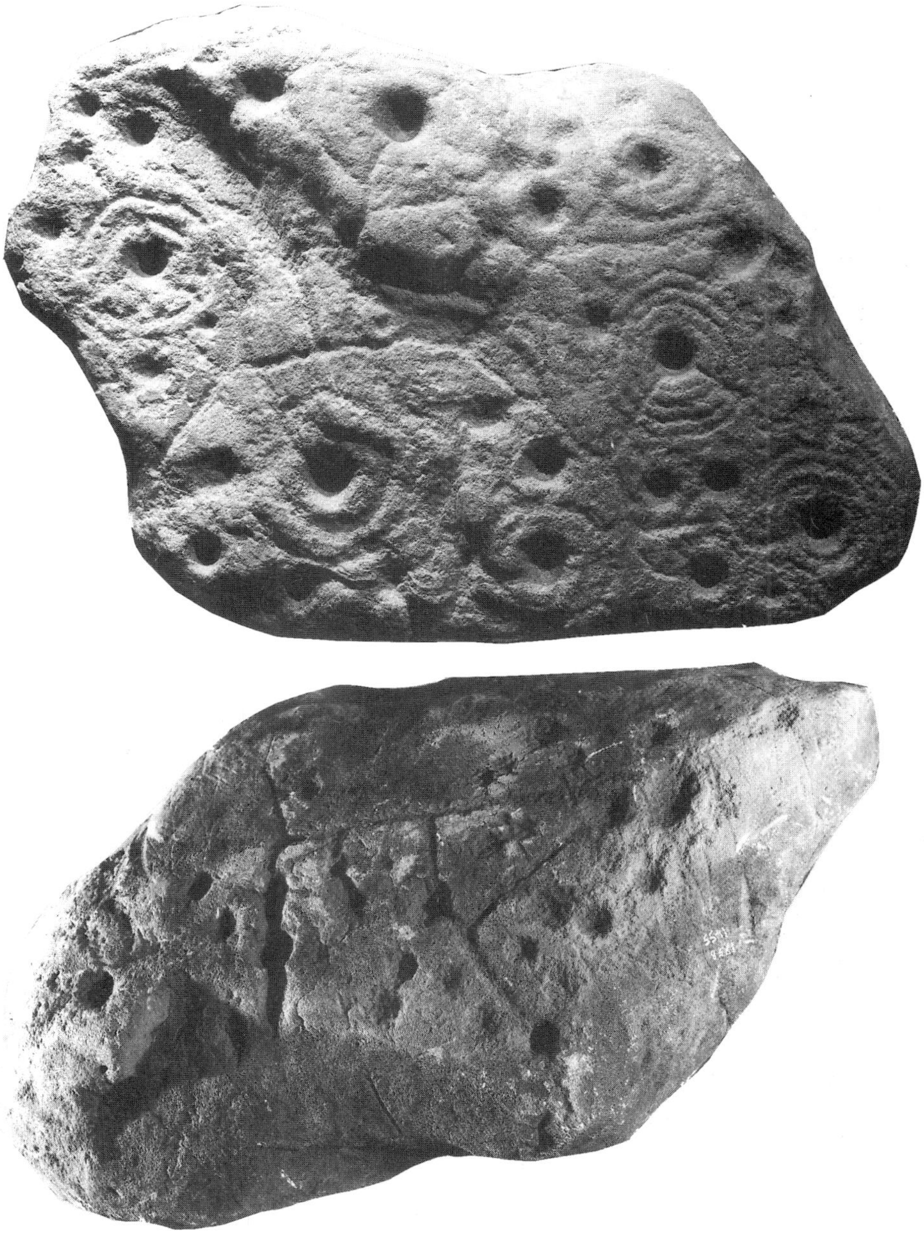

The Gainford Cist Cover

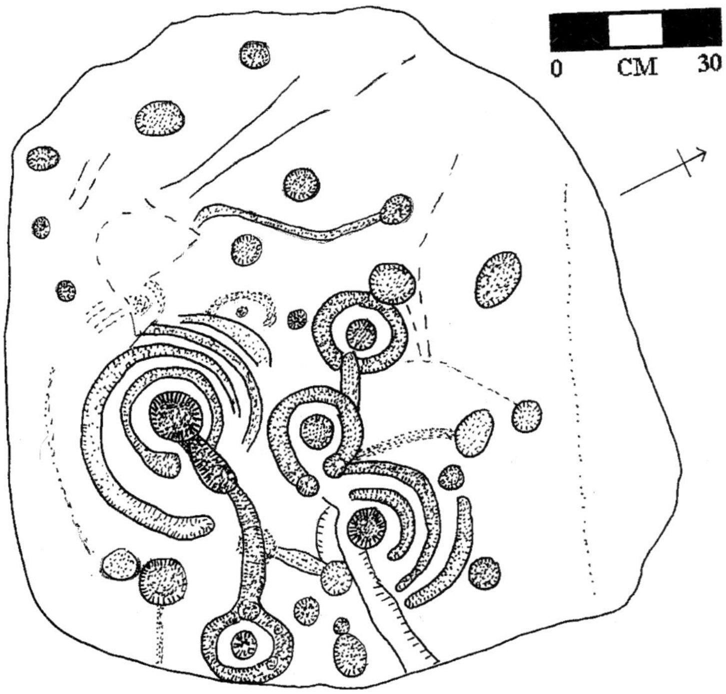
0 CM 30

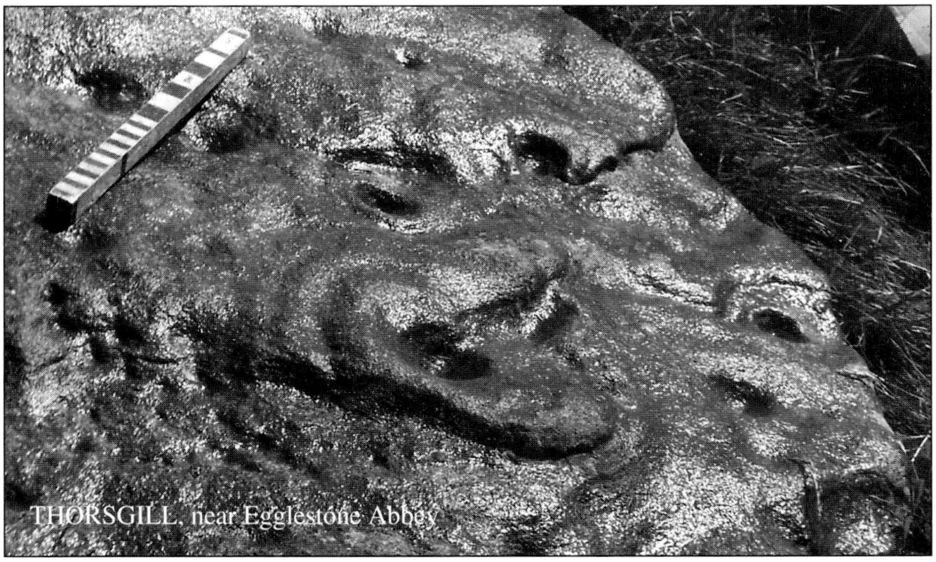
THORSGILL, near Egglestone Abbey

**Feldom slab**: this stone, now in the Bowes Museum, was found beside a tumbled wall in April, 1996. (NZ 1045 0460). Paul Brown rescued it from possible damage.

**The Ravensworth stone** was discovered by the authors in July,1994. It is part of a small, cobbled pavement in front of The Bay Horse Hotel, and it could have come from the moorlands near by, brought in as building material. It is particularly well executed, the concentric rings around the central cup being delicately chipped in close together. Like the stones from Dalton, though, it may have been included within a cist structure.

**The Thorsgill stone** is accessible on the north slope of the Thorsgill Beck opposite Egglestone Abbey. There is a small bridge over the stream on the narrow road from the Abbey, and the rock lies across the north bank, its present location arising from field clearance of the river terrace. Any irregularities in the smooth sandstone have been used in the design. The multiple ring motifs are incomplete, and there are signs that the rock was marked at different times with a slight change in plan. The photograph and drawing illustrate this complexity, and it is interesting to compare it with the rock at Stelling. If this stone comes from a destroyed cairn or cist burial, its position opposite the Abbey gives it a nice sense of place and continuity.

**The Leonard's Cragg stone**, N. Stainmore (NY 82351420)
Reported by Dr. Anthony Flood,M.C., this cup and ring motif was found between the A66 west of North Stainmore and the minor road south that runs from the A66 to Tewfitt Mires. It is located on a sandstone cliff made by 18th. Century quarrying, at its edge. It is embedded, half covered with earth and grass, to the west of Leonard's Cragg Farm. The site is above the 310m contour. The design is three penannulars around a central cup, with an incomplete fourth on the outside, and the drawing is made from a rubbing by Paul Brown. There is a small worn cup 1m from the main motif. A further search has so far not located any others.

Leonard's Cragg, North Stainmore

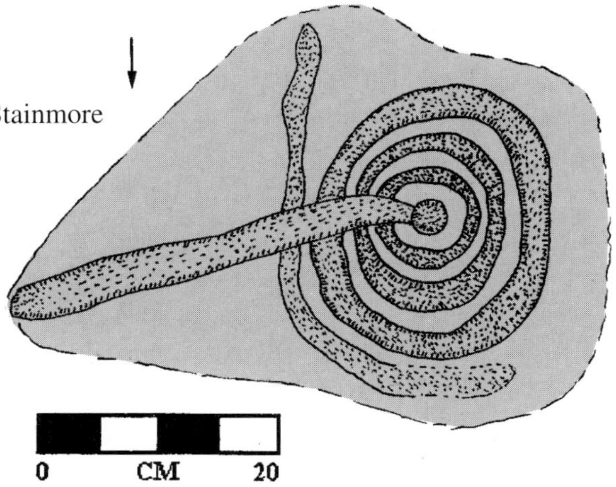

# 8. Swaledale

## HOLGATE

Holgate How has a large round barrow on the summit (SD 067 048, 436m.OD), with extensive views in all directions. Scattered rocks on the grass slopes below this cairn include some with motifs, to the south east of the West House fields. Holgate has three distinct natural zones, marked by green tracks:-

1. The highest tract. At the foot of this first slope are many scattered blocks of stone, none marked.
2. Towards the valley, below the higher green track, is an area with a scatter of much larger earthfast blocks of sandstone, many that bear marks of quarrying, and some of which have prehistoric motifs.
3. Below the lower green track is an area predominantly of rough grass, in which are various earthfast stones some of which are marked, and to the north of which is one of the most interesting designs in the area.

**Rock 1**: On the level ground, where the ground falls away towards the farm road is a large block of stone that has 25 cups of various sizes and depths, concentrated mainly on the SW part.

**Rock 2**: A flat slab has 3 cups and a faint ring.

**Rock 3**: Further north is a large quarried earthfast slab on two levels which carries motifs. A groove from north to south runs the whole width of the rock, passing through a large shallow cup and a larger basin in which water accumulates which may have eroded two other cups. Parallel to this, to the west, is a shorter groove ending in a heart-shaped figure that makes use of a natural rise in the rock surface. Whereas the heart-shape is quite clear, there are some less-obvious signs of working in the form of grooves below it. Parallel to both of these grooves, further to the east, a groove runs from a prominent cup towards the quarried edge of the rock. Wedge marks, fortunately, did not damage it.

**Rock 4**: On the lowest slope, and furthest south, is a flat outcrop with a rounded edge that has three very small cups.

**Rock 5**: A rock with two well-defined cups marks the southern limit of the marked rocks, so we have cup marked stones on the periphery of an area that carries more complex markings to the north.

**Rock 6**: (SD 06740 0426,365m OD) Here the art becomes a little more elaborate. A uniform block of earthfast sandstone, with a slope at the right-hand side, its straight sides are the result of recent quarrying. Wedge marks, which could be on a line of cups, nearly sealed the rock's fate. The design relies on inter-connected cups and grooves for its fluidity. Two cups with single rings have grooves leading from the cups, but the other cup and ring has a groove leading from the ring edge. Inter-connected cups complete the pattern, although two inter-connected cups and a single ring lie outside this (unless they, too, were to be joined). Faint hollows on the rock could be natural. The left-hand side has suffered damage, including erosion, but the figures at the top could be unfinished as the outer penannular stops at a cup. Among the other cups, two have traces of a single ring.

**Rock 7**: (SD 0642 0447, 360 OD) The most elaborate motifs are found on this large, rounded earthfast boulder. It lies a few metres below the squeeze stile through a recent field wall (public footpath). Particularly interesting is the making of enclosures with nothing inside them, and the use of parallel grooves. The drawing 'flattens' the

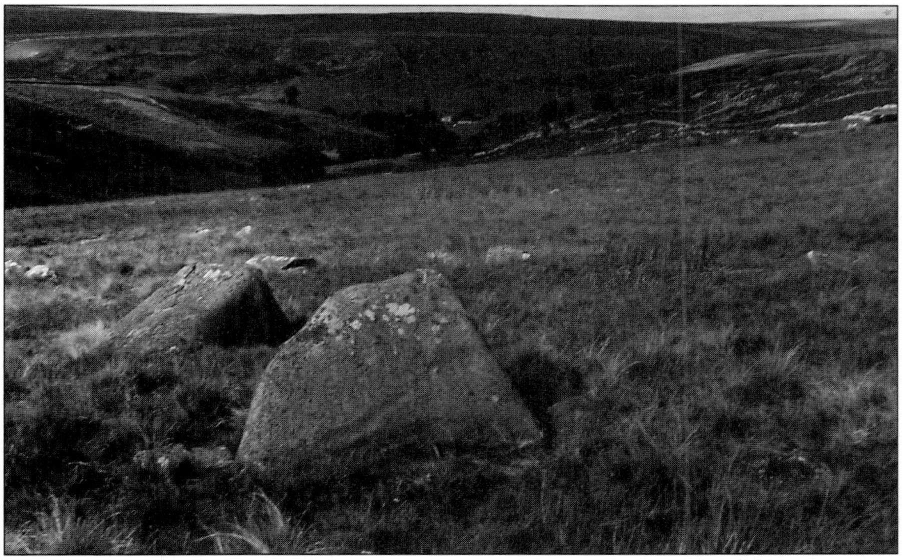

HOLGATE: coarse grassland with scattered rocks, some of which are marked. All the marked rocks are at viewpoints overlooking the valley, with high moorland beyond.

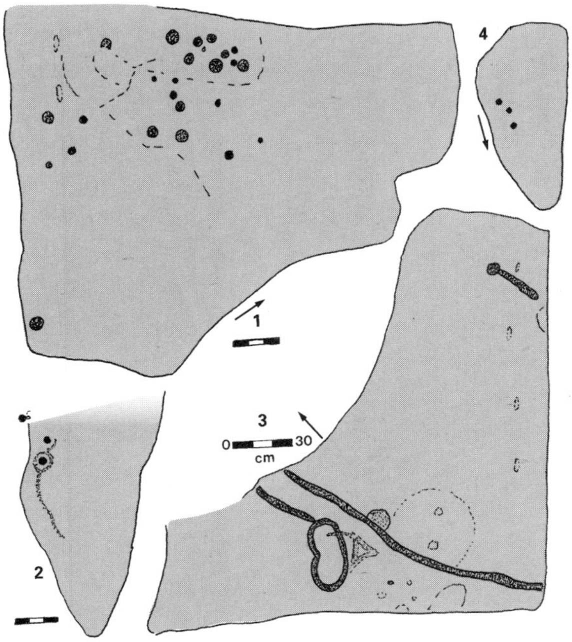


Holgate 1-4

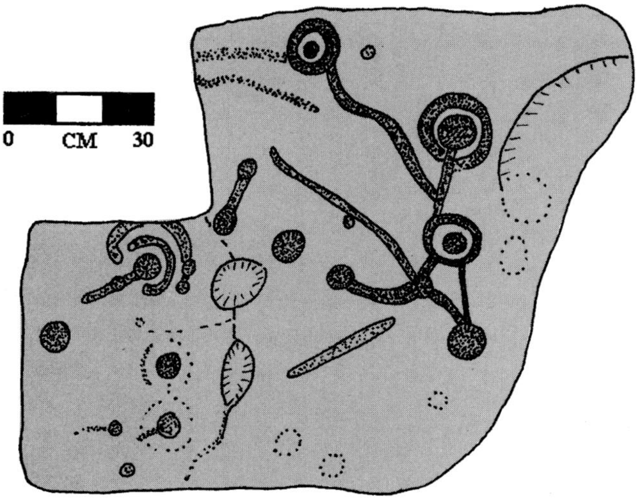


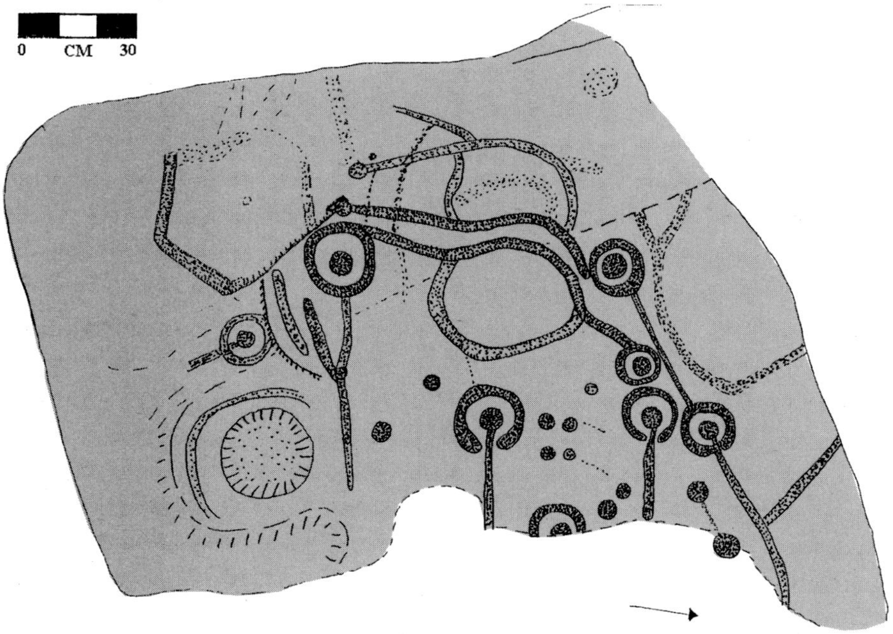


HOLGATE rocks 6 and 7

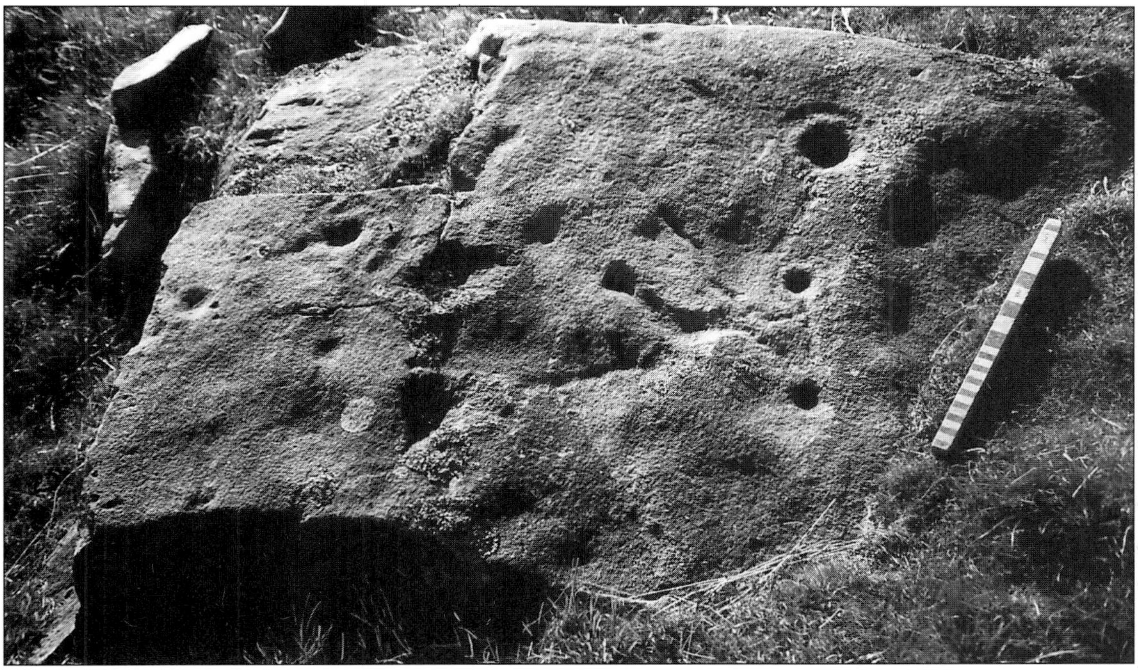

HOLGATE: Rocks 6 (above) and 7

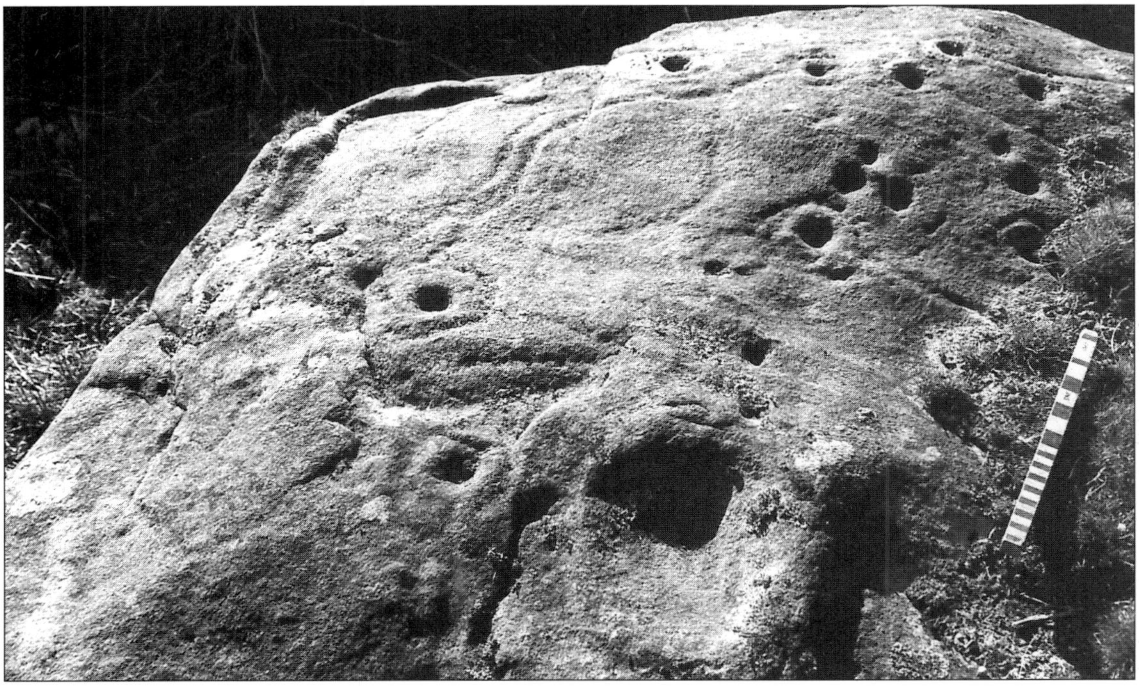

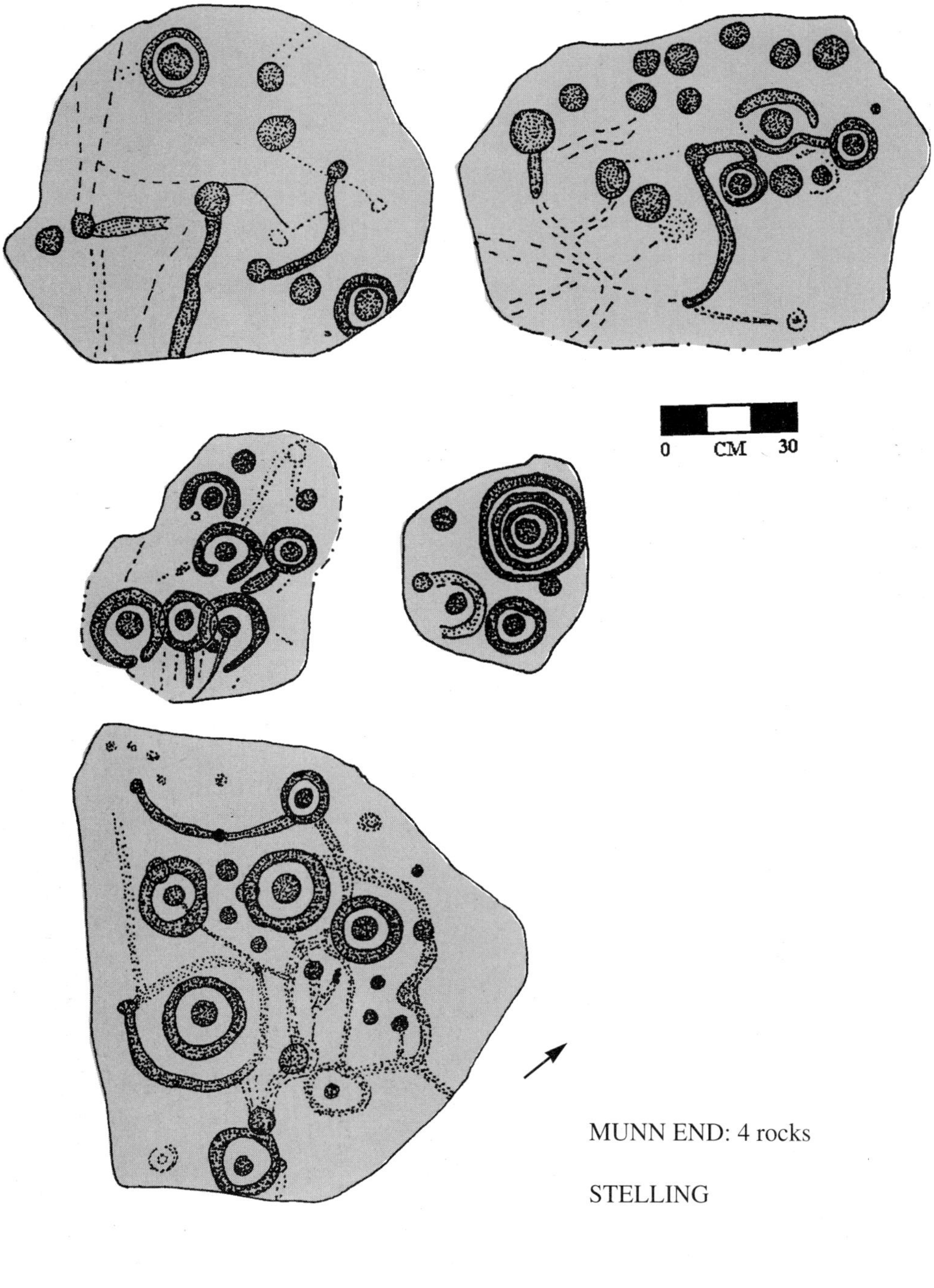


MUNN END: 4 rocks

STELLING

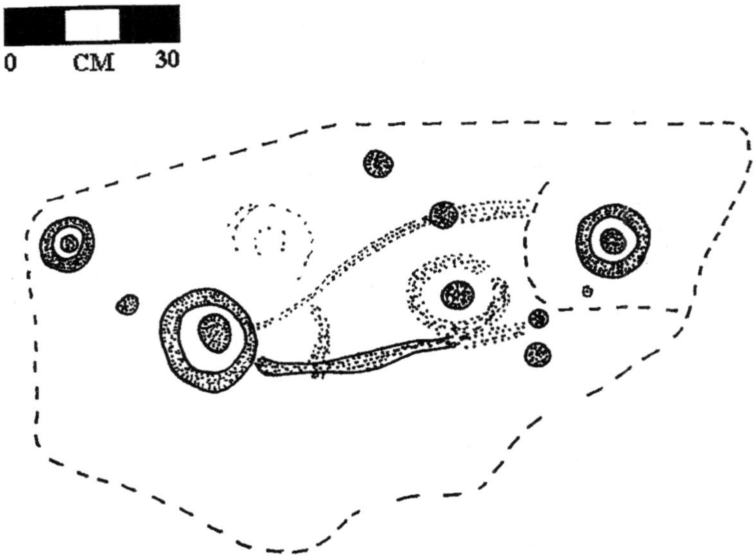


COCK HOW 2

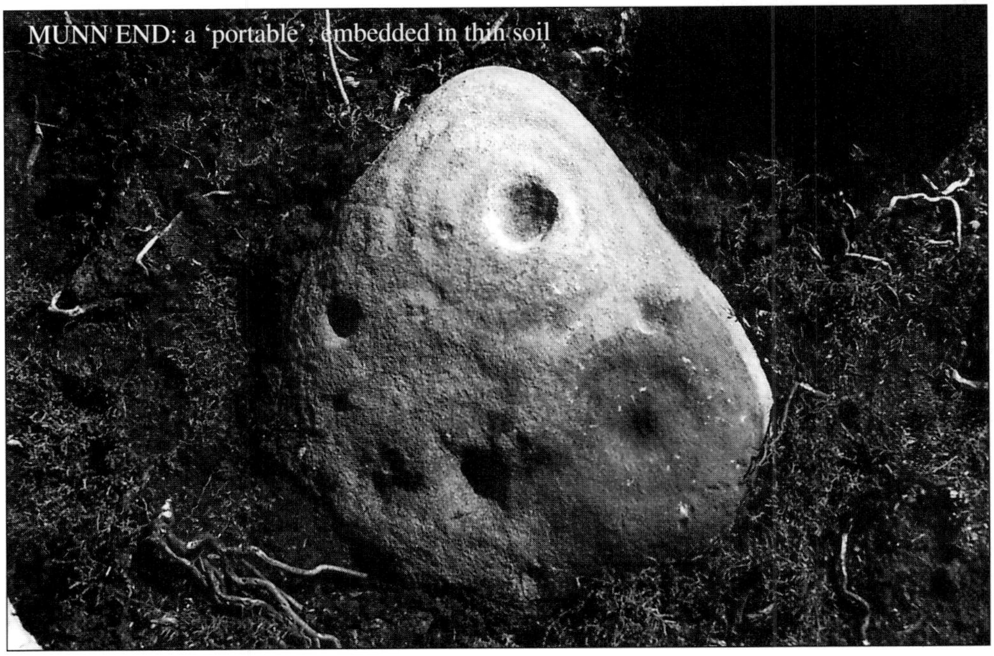

MUNN END: a 'portable', embedded in thin soil

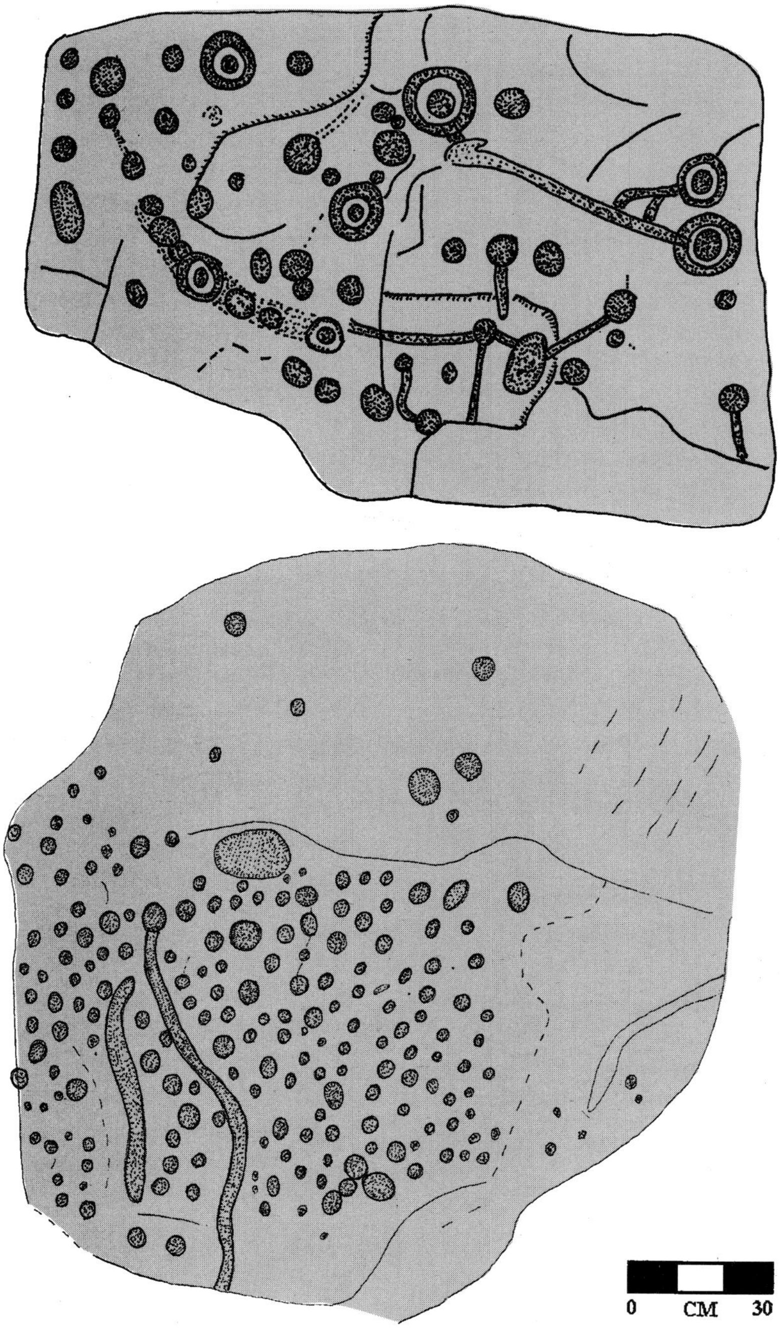


COCK HOW rocks 1 and 3.

rock, which slopes to the north east, drops vertically to the north, and slopes to the south west. On the left, a large natural basin with a natural ridge of stone around it, has been partially enclosed by a groove and brought into the design. The east part of the rock has a grooved enclosure at the centre top, and a series of cups and single rings or penannulars that lead single grooves down the rock. The lines flow on to the west, parallel, linked to cups and to a cup and ring. There are unattached cups also, including pairs, and faint additional grooves. On the north side, a definite and a faint groove veer away from the general trend.

The location of these rocks is dominant in the landscape of the Marske Beck. Unenclosed ancient settlements have been found on Strappan Hill (SD 072 043,365 OD) and above the west slopes of the Marske Beck, on Moresdale Ridge and above Rispy Wood. A long boulder wall or bank leads to an isolated cairn in thick heather above Rispy Wood (SD 05 04).

**Stelling**

Access to the following rock by the general public is not allowed by the farmer.

The rock lies in a field recently cleared of tons of stone. It survives as an earthfast block, left behind by retreating ice, on top of a glacial moraine at the bottom of a valley on the west bank of Dales Beck. Its viewpoint is along the valley floor from a raised position, and it can be seen from high up the valley slopes.

Roughly triangular in shape, it has a fairly even, horizontal surface. The main elements are connecting grooves, some containing cups, a single ring around a cup, with one double ring. The most interesting feature, apart from the pleasant effect of the whole design, is that the markings exhibit a palimpsest. The conception of the final form may have developed over a period of time, and the network of grooves is less emphatic than the ringed figures. In places, cups were there before the grooves were cut through them, and are used to guide the grooves.

## SKELTON MOOR

Skelton Moor, the heather grouse moor above 300m to the west of Marske Beck includes Skelton, Moor House and Telfit Farms. Rocks with cups only and with cups and rings are found at Munn End and below Cock How.

**Munn End**

Three of the four marked rocks occur close together on the same part of the moor, and the other, to the west, is 'portable', possibly from a destroyed monument. All are on the edge of high ground, before it drops away steeply to the Marske valley. None of the rocks is visible from 5m in this heather moorland, and are invisible when the heather grows to its full height. The motifs have survived quarries and mining, but there are many traces of linear low walls and occasional cairns which point to land use in prehistoric times, possibly with an emphasis on control of livestock. The grouse butts make a convenient reference point for those wishing to find the marked rocks. One group lies 100m west of the green track from Skelton to Helwith (SD 081 019, 345m OD).

The location of these three flat earthfasts gives extensive views to the Durham coast, the north and west scarp of the North York Moors, and the Vale of York. The fourth, further west, is a small portable boulder, decorated profusely, and may have been part of a burial cairn. Several small cairns and two ring cairns survive on Munn End.

**Cock How**

Cock How is an isolated round hill, partly heather grouse moor, partly recently improved pasture, to the north of the old road from Richmond to Fremington and Reeth, 3km west of Marske. Two lead veins marked by numerous bell pits and shallow shafts have been heavily exploited by early miners on the south east and the north east slopes of Cock How. Recent field survey by Tim Laurie and aerial photography have defined an extensive co-axial field system of parallel banks which extends across the whole of Cock How and Skelton Moor. This field system is overlain by a later prehistoric sub rectangular enclosure which is likely to be Iron Age.

Three marked rocks have been discovered at NZ085002 (centre): a large boulder, and two small flat earthfast slabs on a slope, with wide views from the rocks. Unfortunately clearance has removed prehistoric field banks, but the marked rocks have been spared.

**Rock 1**: It is difficult to imagine a less likely surface for marking. The sandstone earthfast block is pocked and uneven, but there does not appear to be much other rock in the vicinity. Even so, use has been made of the rock structure, notably in the natural rectangular recessed area (west), through which a faint artificial groove links a series of cups and rings implanted in a natural groove (north) to other cups with grooves leading into the rectangle. Again, cups and a single ring are standard. Because the rock is naturally pitted, it is sometimes difficult to distinguish between natural and artificial.

**Rock 2**: A flat, smooth earthfast block, its long grooves follow established erosion lines.
A cup and single ring is the predominant motif.

**Rock 3**: This outstanding boulder, next to a drystone wall, has its west slope covered with about 200, mostly small, cups and two grooves. A few cups spill over to the east, almost vertical face. The cups at the foot of the western face have clear pick marks, and the rest have been smoothed, most likely by exposure. The cups are not easily visible unless the light is strong and oblique, but in the right conditions, the cups and grooves stand out in a spectacular pitting of the whole surface. One groove begins with a cup mark. At the top of the rock is a large oval cup, contrasting with the others.

None of these rocks is accessible without permission.

**DOWNHOLME**

The village of Downholme lies south and east of the Marske-Skelton area and above the River Swale, near the junction of the B6270 and A6108 roads. After the steep drop to the valley, the landscape rises and falls gently, reaching little over 300m. Old shafts, small woods and rifle ranges lie in open pasture, and in this area, reached by a minor road out of the village, are three marked rocks, centred on Thorn Hill (SE 119 989, 283m OD). The most remarkable of them is a glacial sandstone boulder, which has a triangular or heart shaped groove pecked into it: unique in this region. The boulder is isolated and overlooked by rising ground. The upper surface of this rock has been defaced in antiquity, possibly to remove a more prominent carving. The other rocks are earthfast slabs, one flat and the other tilted, and carry a common local design based on cups, linked cups and grooves. The land here is pasture, with thin soil. “Sourmoor Hill” nearby is probably a comment on the land’s condition. Like many other sites, this is on marginal land, and probably most suitable for hunting. Today this is army land, and a possible round barrow on Thorn Hill has been much spread around by foxhole digging. Traces of field walls, and small clearance cairns can be seen to the east of the plantation at SE 117 987, 280m OD, and a well-preserved series of platform settlements have survived above Sidebank Wood and White Scar. The unenclosed road from Hudswell to Downholme provides a series of splendid viewpoints that overlook the landscape of lower Swaledale and the uplands

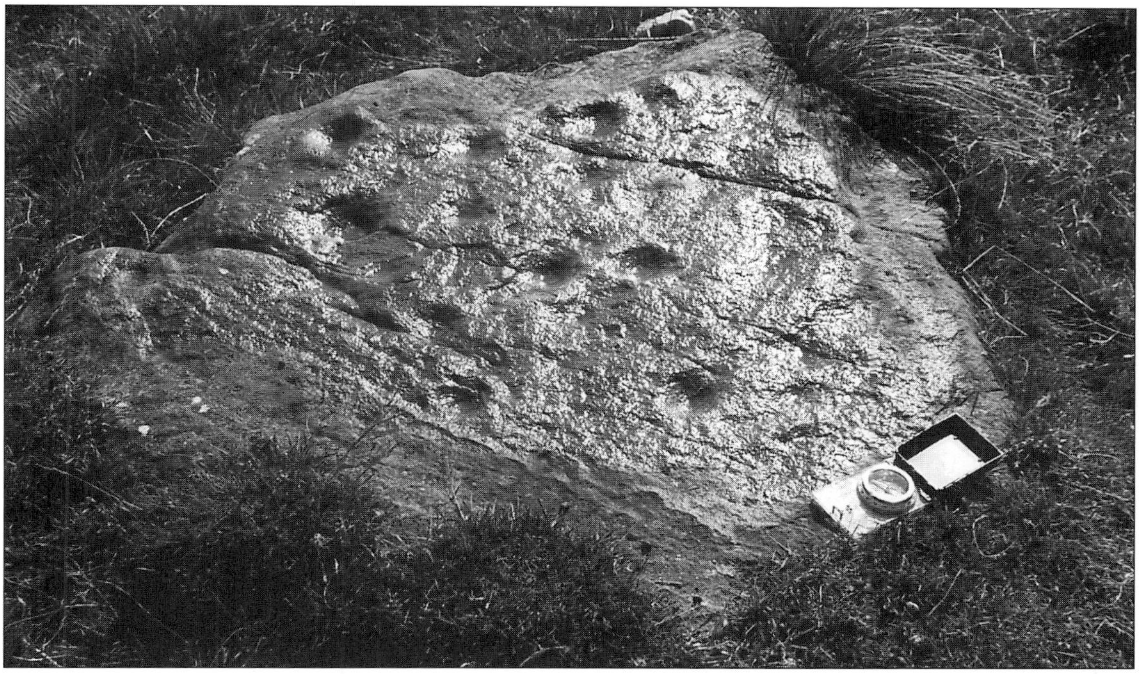

DOWNHOLME: a flat earthfast rock (above) and a large decorated boulder.

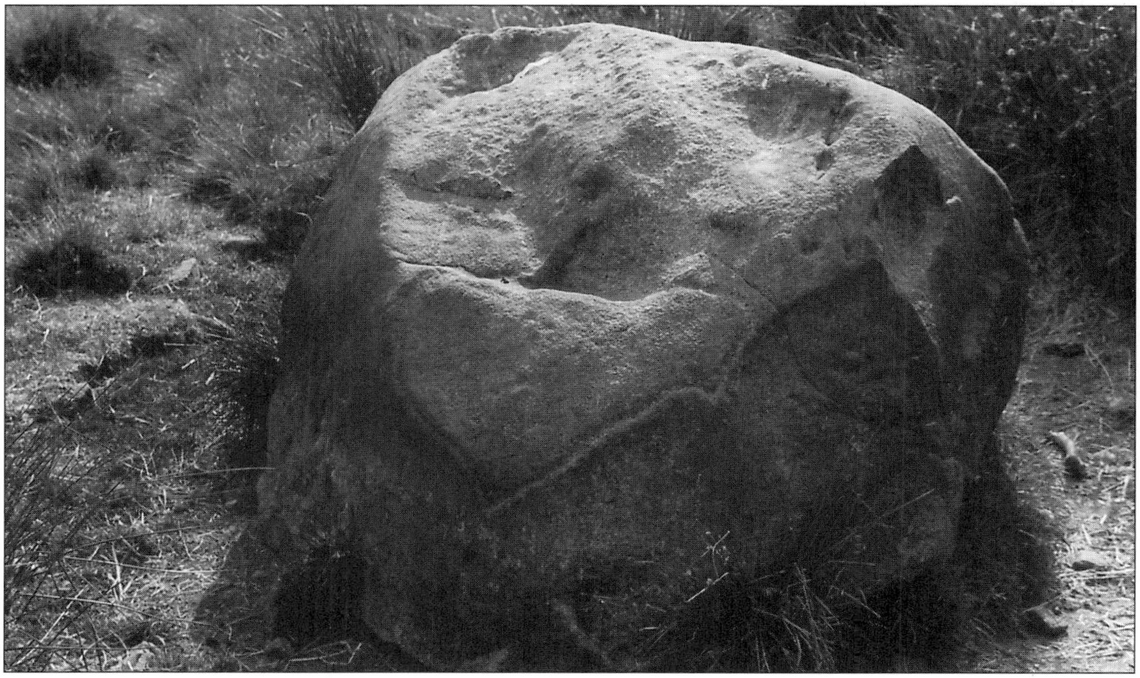

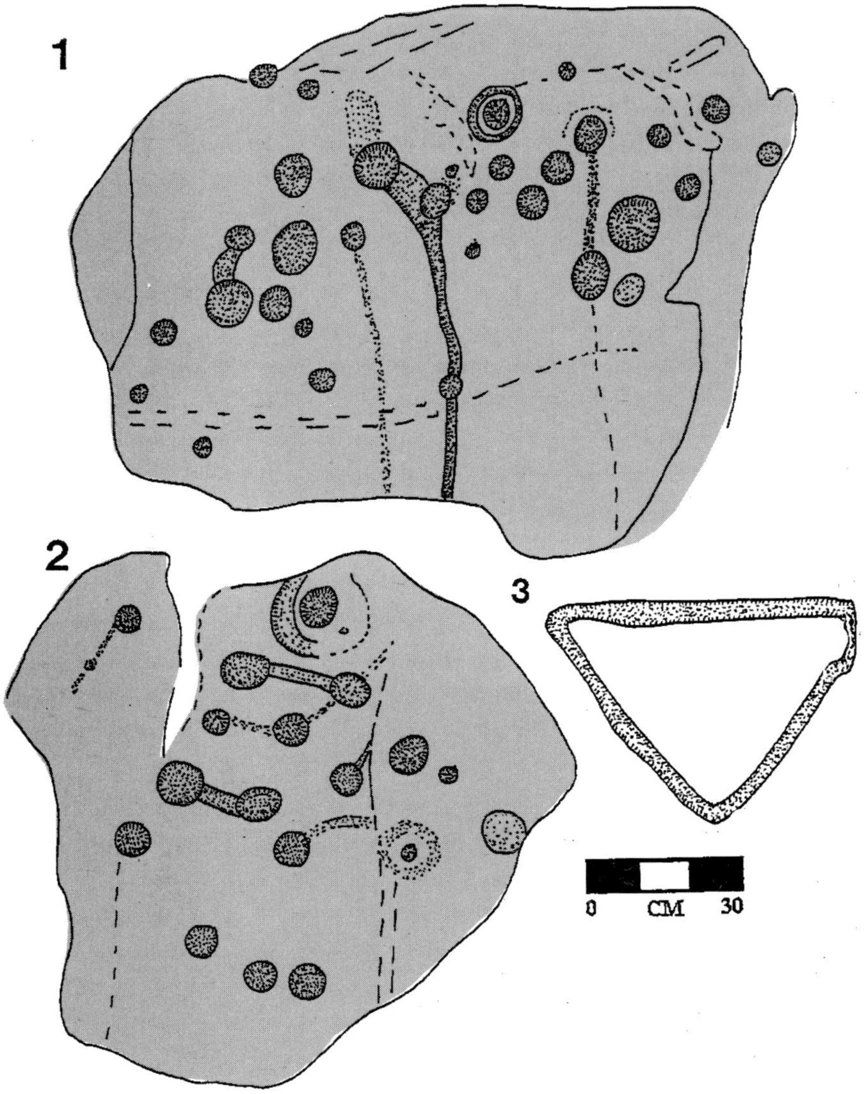


DOWNHOLME

between Swale and Tees, including Copperthwaite, Skelton Moor, Holgate How and Feldom east of Marske Beck.

**JUNIPER GILL**

The cupped standing stone at Juniper Gill is situated on a low col between lower Wensleydale and Swaledale and is a marker on the natural pass on the best and easiest crossing of the Pennines for the traveller on foot from the south and east - the Vale of Mowbray to the north and west - to the Vale of Eden. This route would cross the Juniper Gill Col and the standing stone is the place where the summit of Stainmore first becomes visible through Arkengarthdale across Stainmore Forest. A recently-discovered stone circle at Mudbeck (NY 955 076 385m OD) is at the point where Ray Cross, the Stainmore summit, becomes visible on reaching the watershed between Swale and Tees on the line of one of three of the lowest and easiest crossings of the Northern Pennines. The view is extensive - the Pennine escarpment above the Eden valley can be seen to the north west and the non prehistoric cooling towers of Selby are visible to the south.

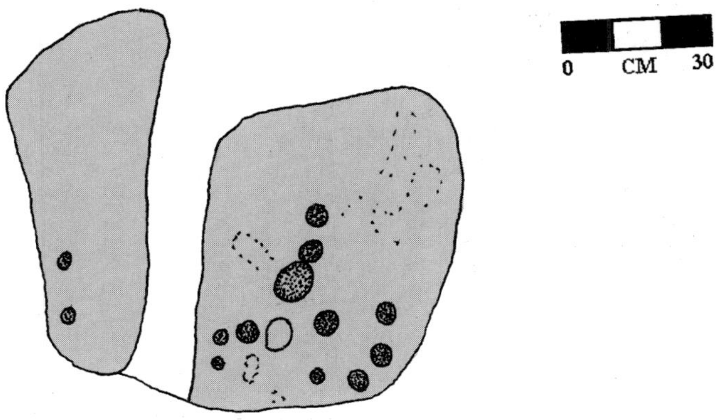


The upper surface of a standing stone at Juniper Gill

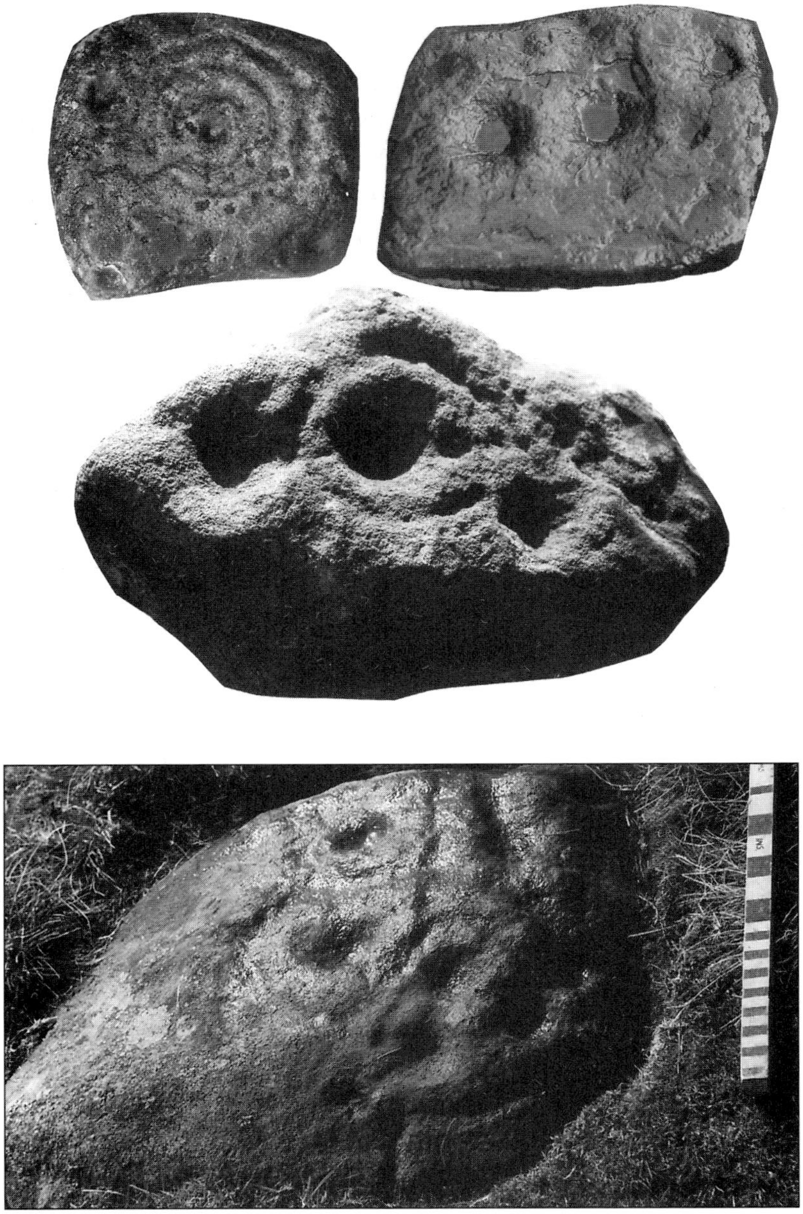

"Portable" stones. The top two are from Dalton, marked on two and three faces.
Centre: a cobble from Barningham, marked on four faces.
Lower: embedded in the top of a cairn above Osmonds Gill.

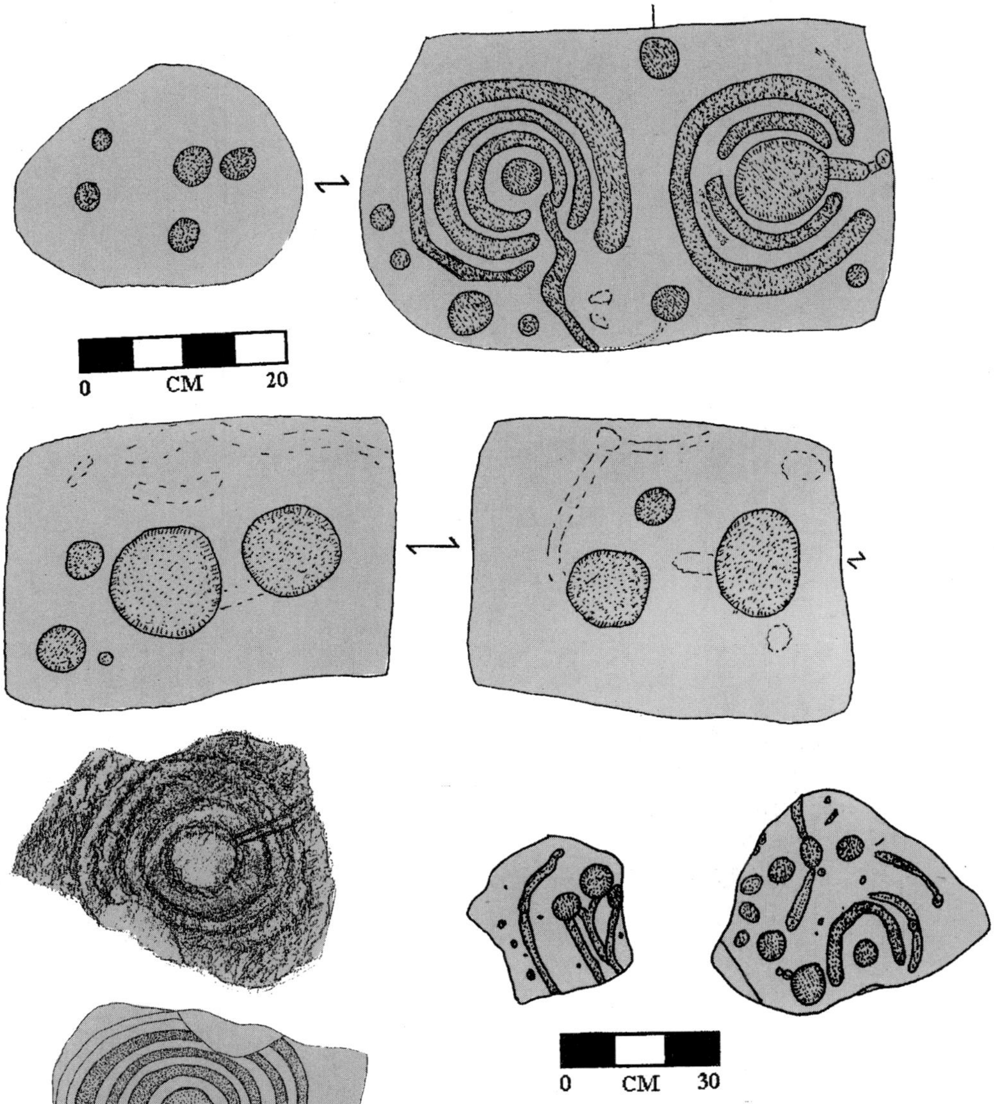


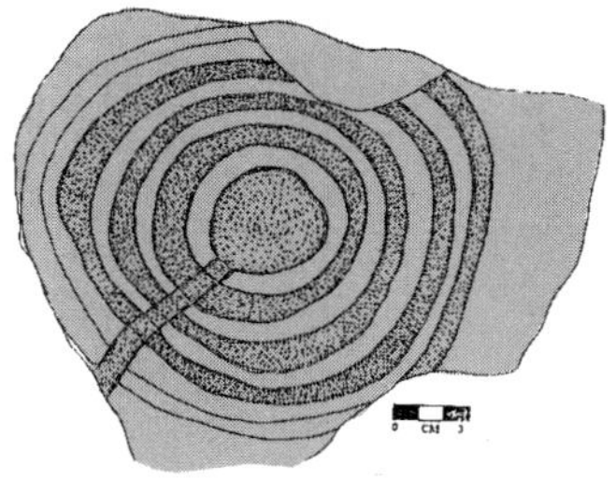

Top: Dalton (3 faces)
Middle: Dalton (2 sides)
LL. A rubbing and a drawing of the Ravensworth stone.
LR. Folly Plantation, Feldom.

# 9. Wensleydale

Addlebrough is a prominent, isolated hill south of Bainbridge, rising to 476m OD, with alternating strata of sandstone, shale and limestone. The summit cliffs formed by the Underset limestone and the summit plateau are littered with erratic blocks of fell sandstone. The less steep slopes are formed by softer shale outcrops, covered with peat and boulder clay to form rough pasture. South of this prominent hill, on its slopes and south across Thornton Mire on Greenber Edge are settlements, marked by low stone walls, and an oval stone barrow. The latter, Stoney Raise cairn, the largest Prehistoric structure in the North Pennines, 38m x 28m, had hundreds of loads of stone removed from it in 1805. At a lower level than Addlebrough and to the SE is the Castle Dyke henge. There is a prehistoric presence, therefore, that includes not only Iron age or later houses and stockyards, but early prehistoric ritual and burial. There are Neolithic settlements on the Semerwater Lake edge. To the west, on Scout Crag above Bardale there is a fine ring cairn with a central burial mound, first noted by David Hall. On the long ridge which forms the western flank of Raydale, on a spur named Crag is a 9m diameter undisturbed round barrow found by Mrs. Elizabeth Wright (SD 904 877, 505m OD), from the molehills of which she collected sherds of food vessel. It is within a setting of late Neolithic/early Bronze Age sites that Addlebrough must be considered. The summit cairn on Addlebrough is turf covered, in which sandstone slabs are set, four of which have simple cups, one including a single ring. The cairn commands wide views in all directions except to lower ground to the south and south west. Semerwater is close below the cairn but not visible from it.

The significance of marked stones on cairns, which may be contemporary with the cairn's construction, re-used in its making, or later, has already been noted in the cairns of Barningham Moor. Fortunately, the site is owned by the National Trust, although there is no footpath to the summit. There are public footpaths that are close to settlements and the henge, but access is on private land. The choice of cup marked stones on such a prominent landmark as the cairn gives them an importance beyond their simplicity. The settlements are dry stone walls that form small enclosures for stock, and the foundations of round houses that could support a roof with thatch, but they are certainly later than the cairn. Despite searches, no other undisputed cupped stones have been found on the summit, although there is no shortage of suitable rock surfaces, since many erratic fell sandstone blocks litter the surface. A single possible cup marked stone has been noted to the SSE of the summit cairn, and a rock with several cups has recently been noticed on Thornton Rust Moor near the Dovestones.

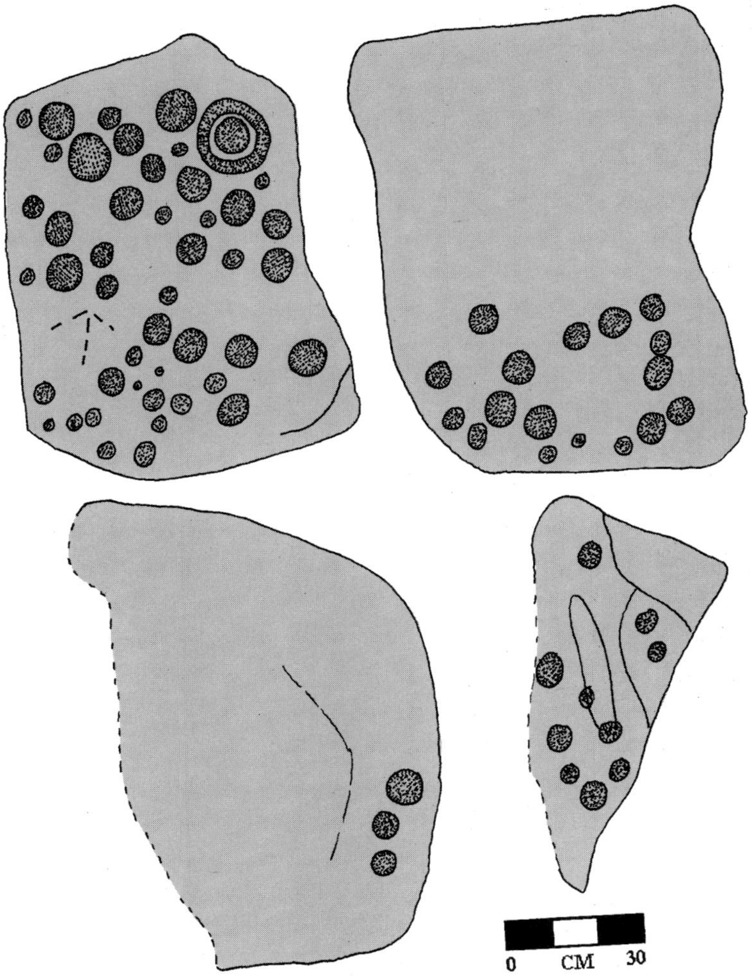


Four marked rocks on the Addlebrough Cairn

# 10. The early hunters and pastoral farmers in the rock art areas

At Hard Hill some 3km ESE of the source of the Tees, at 685m OD, a group of 7 flint artefacts has been collected over 3 years from the eroding face of a residual mound of blanket peat which once covered the whole area. Associated with them, 1m above the mineral soil at the base of the peat, fragments of two horns were found, probably belonging to the Urus species of oxen. These flints and horns were found at a level that has been dated from the pollen content in the whole deposit to a period known as the Atlantic or Climatic Optimum, the period of greatest warmth and 'oceanic' wetness, from approximately 7,000 years ago when a marked increase in the growth of alder trees witnessed a change from cool, dry conditions to 5,000 years ago when elm decline heralded a change to a cool 'oceanic' climate with the fluctuating temperatures that we experience today.

We know then that there were hunters in the High Pennines approximately 5,000 years ago when in other parts of Britain cup marks were being made below earthen barrows and on some rock surfaces. No cup marks or cup and ring marks have been found in Upper Teesdale at the Hard Hill site, but many scatters of flints similar to the Hard Hill flints have been found on river terraces and high moorland slopes lower down the Tees valley and in Swaledale close to rock markings. Among the flints from Hard Hill are two minute barbs of composite arrow points, see illustration page 6.

As you consider such tiny arrow points and barbs, you may well wonder how these Middle Stone Age hunters were able to face wild cattle with the sharpest and longest horns! Yet there is no doubt that all over the world hunters have used such weapons, and for such a considerable time, from 10,000 - 5,000 years ago in Britain.

About 6,500 years ago the earliest 'pastoralist' farmers arrived. The main change in their way of life was the new skill with which they could control their food supply by herding animals and pasturing them. They brought a different kind of technology with them that we can detect in many artefact scatters. They used 'pressure flaking' to produce high quality leaf-shaped and barb and tang arrow points of the Neolithic and Early Bronze Age.

For at least a thousand years, after about 6,500 years ago, Mesolithic and Neolithic cultures existed in Northern England, and where these two cultures meet, from the evidence of the artefacts they left behind, is where we find much of the rock art. These places therefore link time and place between developing farming communities and their aboriginal ancestors. This does not mean that both groups made the markings, but it does mean that they used the same places in the landscape for their activities. We shall now look a little closer at this.

The hunter groups that first used the area most likely would have been based at the coast. Many such bases have been drowned by rising sea levels since then. From the available evidence, the whole of Wensleydale, Swaledale, Teesdale and Weardale was a pristine wilderness visited only occasionally by hunters, and they developed a clear preference for sheltered gravel terraces close to the main rivers, their main base camps. Small, opportunistic hunting camps have been found on high slopes, now open moorland, close to watershed springs, south-facing and commanding wide views - good vantage points from which game herds could be observed and close to water for the immediate needs of the group at rest. Rock art is found at the same locations and nearby. If one 'use' of rock art is to define territory, these sites could be territorial limits.

However, rock art is not at precisely the same locations as these early hunting camps, and although the markings are located at sites with wide views, riverside bluffs and high, open terraces of the dale sides, they show no preference for south-facing aspects. They do share the same elevation and are close to Mesolithic sites. Neither has been found any distance from rivers or springs at intermediate levels.

***Stone tools***

As the only evidence for these early hunting groups comes from surface scatters of flint and chert, the material used for making them, we shall look at this evidence.

***Flint***

Flint is a form of silica, and occurs naturally as nodules in chalk, on the coast, or within glacial drift. The nearest sources would be from glacial clay with flints deposits within crevices in the Magnesian Limestone on the Durham coast. Early hunters using camp sites on the Pennines also used white flint, from the Yorkshire Wolds.

Flint breaks with a conchoidal fracture like broken glass, and flakes of flint are translucent, often coloured with minerals. The nodules are covered with a "skin"' (cortex), which needs to be removed to reach the clear flint. After exposure it becomes less brittle, and after a while it becomes 'patinated' opaque, dirty white or grey, like old milk. As it does not occur naturally in the area, it has all been brought here. Flint blades are long flakes with a length to breadth ratio in excess of $2^1/_2$ to 1.

***Chert***

Chert is tabular silica, and occurs stratified in local Pennine country rocks and in glacial drift and river gravels. Water-transported, rounded cobbles were preferred to chert quarried from outcrop on the Dale sides, which is flawed by frost action. Fine-grained black chert of local river gravel origin occurs on almost all sites of all periods. In the process of tool making, the outer skin or cortex of the flint nodule was removed, and flakes from the cortex were used to make scrapers, awls and other general tools. Hunters used flint barbed arrows to kill their prey, they prepared flint flakes to skin, cut the meat, scrape skins before curing and to bore holes through the skins to make clothes and tent covers. Mesolithic people would produce the maximum number of blades from a nodule, and there would be little waste. Blades were pressed or struck by direct or indirect percussion after a suitable 'platform' had been made. Each blade then removed was triangular in section with a clear ridge.

Microliths are very small barbs of triangular or other preferred shape prepared from flint blades for fixing with birch resin within grooves along the shafts of arrows or spears. They were also used to form the cutting edge of knives as shown on the illustration, page 6.

# 11. The state of the art: Recent research into rock art

The end of this book is a good place to review just how this survey has added to the information on, and thoughts about, prehistoric Rock Art.

We begin by stating some of the things that we do know:

1. All rock art is on fell sandstone in this region.
2. Most motifs are on glacially-transported earthfast or outcrop rock, and the rest are associated with monuments such as cairns.
3. Marks are made by using a hard stone chisel, probably impacted.
4. Rock art is sited on prominent viewpoints, or on elevated slopes with wide views to the horizon.
5. It mainly occupies marginal land overlooking more fertile areas, especially the great river valleys.
6. It is occasionally found in cairns, on cairns, and in a few places it is located on low-walled enclosures or boundary walls of uncertain date. With the possible exception of the very slight enclosures on Washbeck Green and below Eel Hill on Barningham Moor, all enclosures and field boundaries are almost certainly later than the rock art. The earliest enclosures are of 'stone dump' construction. Some are close to springs and other special places in the landscape.
7. In many of the areas where art is found, there are lithic scatters of earlier peoples, and hunters and pastoralist farmers chose the same areas for their activities.
8. At Witton Gilbert we have an eccavated site that provides a late Neolithic/Early Bronze Age date for sealed-in cremation burials, and decorated slabs made specially for the burial ritual.
9. Where marked rocks are found in the more fertile areas, the valleys and river terraces, they appear to have a ritual function rather than a significant place in the landscape. The lack of care in past recording of these sites causes problems of interpretation.
10. Of the symbols and motifs themselves, it can be said they are all abstract, and that the people who made them managed to produce a wide variety of motifs from simple symbols.
11. A consideration of the frequency of cups, cups and groove and concentric circles indicates a grouping of concentric circles at the centre of marked rock concentrations in the Gayles and Barningham areas. Whereas simple cups may also appear at the centre of concentrations of marked rocks, concentric circles do not appear on the periphery. Single ring motifs appear on the edges of major groups and on rocks remote from the main dales, such as Holgate, Munn End and Deepdale.

Now to some of the things we don't know about this region:

1. How the symbols originated.
2. What they meant to the people who used them.
3. When they were made, and for how long they were relevent.

How does all this fit in with the British scene? Most rock art is on marginal land, overlooking fertile areas. There is agreement among archaeologists that the people who made the motifs were not static, arable farmers, but people whose lives incorporated a great deal of mobility. Most rock art is at important viewpoints, and visibility from the art was more important than being able to see the rocks from a distance. Most blend into the landscape so well that they are not

| | |
|---|---|
| Coggins, D., Laurie, T.C. . and Young, R. | 1985. The late Upper Palaeolithic and Mesolithic of the North Pennines in The Mesolithic in Europe (Ed. Bonsall, S.). Edinburgh. |
| Fleming, A., and Laurie,T.C. | 1985-1994. The Swaledale Ancient Land Boundaries project. Interim reports. Unpublished. Yorkshire Dales National Park. |
| Laurie, T.C. | 1985. Early land divisions and settlement in Swaledale and on the eastern approaches to the Stainmore Pass over the north Pennines. In Spratt, D. and Burgess, C. (eds) Upland Settlement in Britain. Oxford. BAR 143. |


***Articles with specific local interest:***


| | |
|---|---|
| Feather, S. | 1967. YAJ 42,111 |
| Feather, S. | 1968. Romaldkirk Moor, YAJ 42,395 |
| Feather, S. | 1968. Blake Hill, Briar Dykes, YAJ 42,242 |
| Feather, S. | 1972. Feldom YAJ 42 |
| Feather, S. | Blake Hill YAJ 50,8 |
| Feather, S. | High Hag YAJ 52,179 |
| Feather, S. | 1981. Feldom YAJ 53 |
| Harding, A.F. | 1987. Recent Acquisitions by the Old Fulling Museum Of Archaeology, Durham, DAJ 3 |
| Laurie, T.C., and Minnitt, R. | 1993. Wensleydale: an Archaeological Survey of Semerwater, Addlebrough and the Stake Road. Prospectus for the Prehistoric Society visit to Ripon. |
| Pickin, J. | 1992. A Prehistoric Boulder from Witton Gilbert, County Durham. DAJ 8. |


FORTHCOMING:
The full report on the Witton Gilbert cist excavation will be a landmark. The Director is Fiona Baker, the Site Supervisor James Wright. The excavation was an official collaboration with Durham County Council, whose Archaeologist is Niall Hammond, and with Professor Anthony F. Harding of the University of Durham Department of Archaeology, where post-excavation analysis of the finds is being undertaken.

# Acknowledgements

The manuscript was typed for publication by Stan Beckensall, with the voluntary help of the Tynedale Business Centre, Hexham, supervised by Stephen Hope. All drawings, photographs, and maps were produced by Stan Beckensall, the latter with help from the Ministry of Defence and English Heritage. Thanks are due to Durham County Council, especially Niall Hammond and to Ros Nichol and Tom Gledhill for specific work on Barningham Moor and general assistance. Other sources are acknowledged in the text.

Access to sites has been with the consent of landowners, tenants, gamekeepers and Range Wardens.

The text is the result of close co-operation between Tim Laurie and Stan Beckensall. Credit for the archaeological background material and for the discovery or recording of most of the sites goes to Tim Laurie. Stan Beckensall's work has concentrated on recording the panels of rock art and describing them within the context of other British rock art.

In addition to, and including individuals named in the text, we are grateful to the following who have contributed to the discovery of marked rocks:

Knitsley: Mr. Dent
Witton Gilbert: Mr. R. Geddes, Mr. Holmes, Mr. J.F.Stevenson, Durham University Department of Archaeology.
Aske Moor to Dousgill: Mr. T.C.Laurie, Mr. S. Feather, Mr. and Mrs. C. Stafford, Mr. J.Blackburn, Mr. P. Brown, Ms. B. Mclean, Mr. Merryn Watson of Newsham.
Barningham Moor: Mr. T.C. Laurie, Mr. P. Brown, Mr. J. Pickin, Ms. B.Mclean, Mr. R. Johnson and son.
Deepdale: Mr. D. Coggins, Mr. P. Brown.
Cotherstone Moor: Mr. D. Coggins, Ms. L. Gidney, T.C. Laurie, Mr. P. Brown
Blake Hill to Eggleston: Mr. D. Coggins, Dr. K. Fairless, Mr. J. Pickin, Mr. P. Brown, Ms. B. Mclean, Mr. M. Gibbs
Eggleston: Mr. P. Brown, Ms. B. Mclean, Mr. M. Gibbs
Holgate: Mr. T.C. Laurie
Stelling, Skelton and Cock How: Mr. T.C. Laurie
Downholme: Mr.T.C.Laurie
Juniper Gill and Wensleydale: Mr. T.C. Laurie

Council for British Archaelogy for a contribution towards publication costs.

The British Museum for permission to reproduce John Sell Cotman's watercolour - Greta Bridge (page 8).

Leeds City Art Galleries for permission to produce John Sell Cotman's watercolour - Barnard Castle from Towler Hill (page 10).

# The Authors

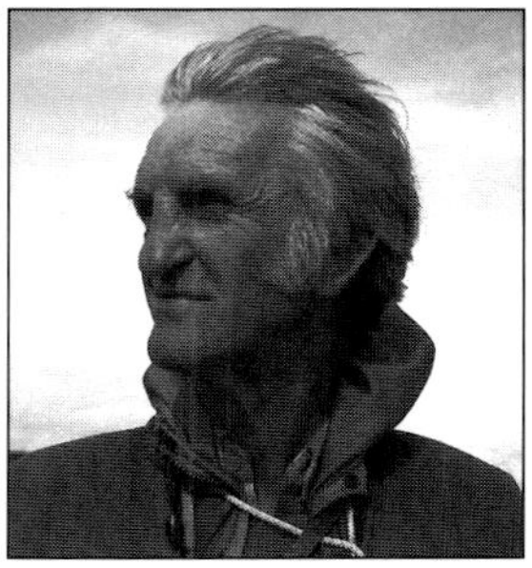

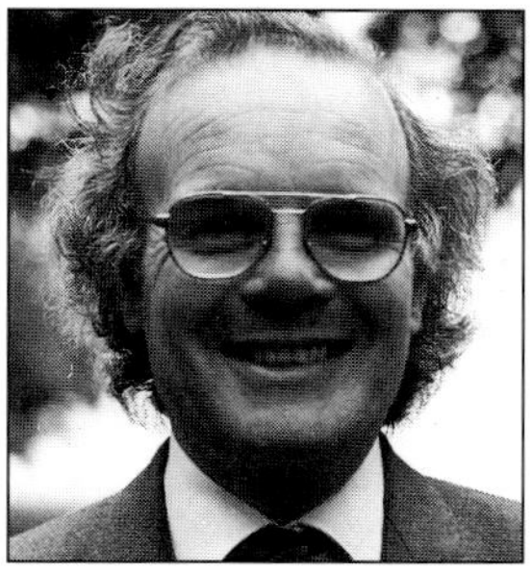

**TIM LAURIE** is a Quantity Surveyor who has worked in the North East for thirty years. During the same period he has been actively engaged as an independent archaeologist in the initial recognition, field survey and interpretation of archaeological sites of all periods in the landscape of Wensleydale, Swaledale, and especially of the uplands between Tees and Swale.

He is co-director, with Andrew Fleming, of the Swaledale Ancient Land Boundaries Project, which is a research programme concerned with the survey and investigation of extensive prehistoric field boundary systems and settlements in Swaledale. This work has been carried out with financial support from the Yorkshire Dales National Park.

He is also a part-time extra-mural lecturer with the University of Leeds, and has given evening classes on field archaeology in the North Pennines over many years.

He has a special interest in the discovery and recording of the evidence for the earliest post glacial and Middle Stone Age (Mesolithic) human occupation of the area. A theme central to this book is the continuity of the occupation of sheltered riverside terraces and high moorland slopes by the earliest aboriginal hunter groups and by the first pastoralist farmers in the area, who are now considered to have made the rock markings.

**STAN BECKENSALL**, now retired, has been a professional teacher all his life, as a head of English in High Schools in Sussex and Malta, as a Senior English lecturer at Alnwick College of Education, and as a head in Northumberland Middle Schools. He has published plays, broadcast some of these with young people, and produced many programmes for the Hexham Abbey Festival. His work in archaeology began as a member of the Research Committee of the Sussex Archaeological Society, and he directed the important excavation of Money Mound in the Central Weald. His most important excavation in Northumberland has been the excavation of cairns at Blawearie, Old Bewick, published by the Prehistoric Society in 1997. He is a fellow of the Society of Antiquaries of Scotland and London, and a member of the International Committee on Rock Art, ICOMOS-CAR.

He has published 15 books and booklets, that include Rock Art, Field and Place Names, Archaeology and Local History, and Drama. At present he is working voluntarily with the Northumberland National Park's Ingram and Upper Breamish Landscape project, directed by the University of Durham's Archaeological Service.

# Location map showing the areas covered by this book

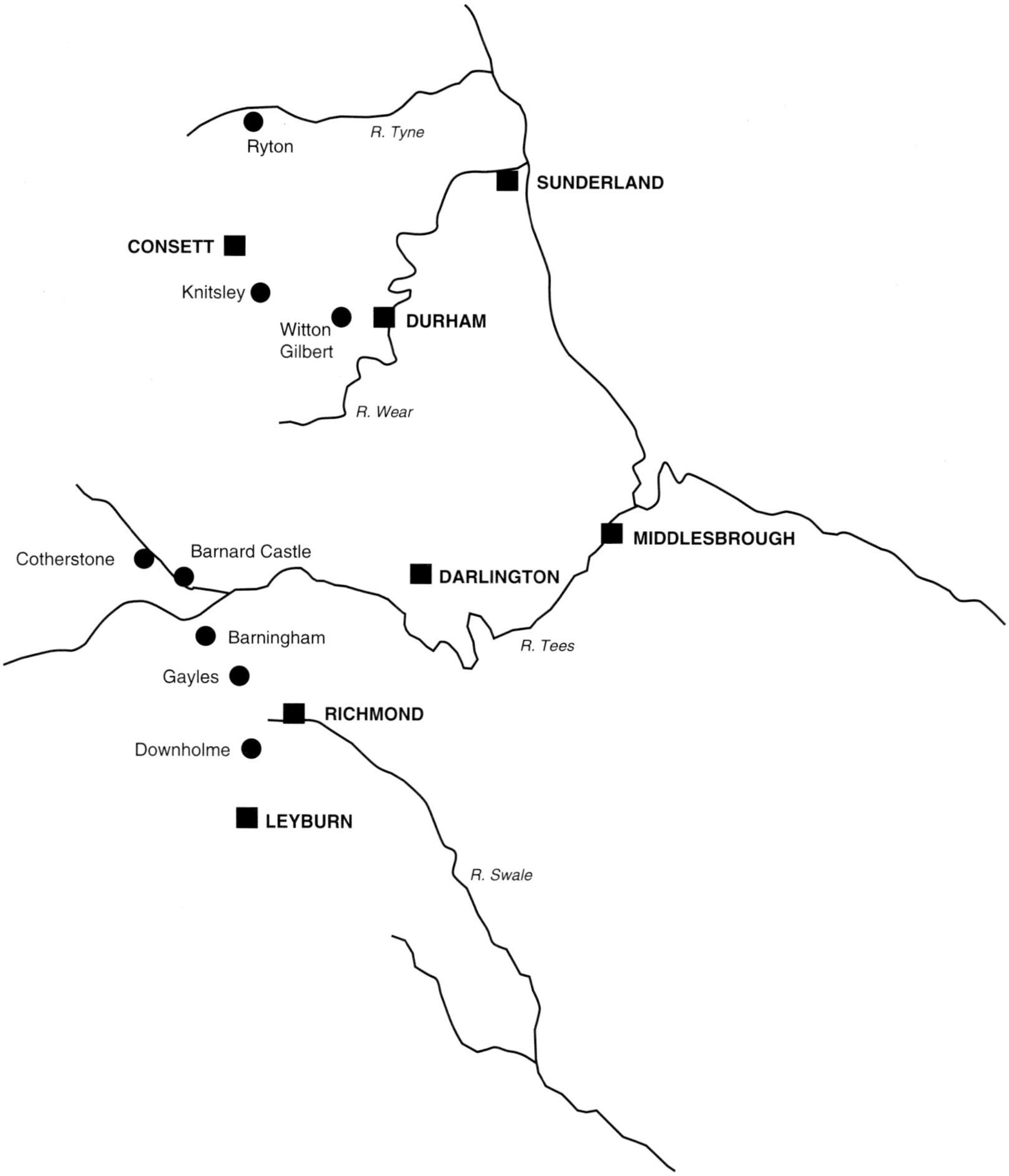